VOLUME III
The Bristol Rovers Archive

Keith Brookman

Copyright © 2022 by Keith Brookman

All rights reserved. No part of this book may be reproduced in any form on by an electronic or mechanical means, including information storage and retrieval systems, without permission in writing from the author, except by a reviewer who may quote brief passages in a review.

Every effort has been made to trace or contact all copyright holders. The author will be pleased to make good any omissions or rectify any mistakes brought to their attention at the earliest opportunity.

ISBN 978-1-8381676-5-3

Typeset by The Logical Choice, Newquay

Printed by TJ Books, Padstow

First edition 2022

Preface

It's been nine years since the publication of the second volume of the Bristol Rovers Archive and, to be honest, I didn't think there would be any more! This third volume covers five years, from 2001 through to 2006 and takes in 100 images that it is hoped will jog a few memories and make it an enjoyable journey through what was not a very successful period in the history of our club.

So why, you may ask, bother with those five years? Well, for the sake of continuity and for my own satisfaction in producing another volume I guess is the answer.

It also has a great deal to do with the Bristol Rovers Supporters Club, an organisation of which I am now secretary. The hard working committee are always looking at new ways of generating income in order to assist the Football Club in any way it can with specific projects.

I offered to self publish this volume of photos and reports at no cost to the Supporters Club, with the proviso that it costs me nothing as well. Once all my costs have been covered, any profit will be donated to the Supporters Club. With a limited print run, I hope that sales will generate a four figure sum for their coffers.

Whilst I have provided the words, the images will also provoke memories and for that I have to thank photographers Alan Marshall, Neil Brookman and Jeff Davis who have all, at one time or another, taken action images of Bristol Rovers on matchdays.

Writing the articles for this publication has brought back many memories from a period of time when I was employed as the Football Club's programme editor and has also inspired me to complete a fourth volume in this series, which will see the light of day if this one is a success!

Thanks to all who purchase a copy of this volume; I hope you enjoy the memories

Gerry Returns

Garry Thompson, caretaker manager for the second half of the 2000/01 campaign, was tipped to be appointed manager on a permanent basis once the final ball of an extremely disappointing season had been kicked.

However, on May 23rd it was reported that 'Tommo' was not going to get the manager's job though he was offered a two year deal as assistant manager. At the time of that announcement, he had no one to assist, though there was speculation that the new boss would come from the following list of suspects; Colin Lee, Brian Little, Ray Graydon, John Rudge, Steve Cotterill and Kenny Hibbitt.

It was, of course, no surprise that none of the aforementioned candidates actually landed the job. Instead, it went to former boss Gerry Francis, who returned to the club he left in 1991. The former England skipper had planned to take a break from the game but was persuaded to take on the challenge of leading Rovers out of the Third Division at the first time of asking.

At the press conference to announce his return, held on June 26th, Francis explained the reasons for his return; 'When I stood down at QPR back in February, I set out my summer to go away with the kids, have a few things done at home and I really didn't think I would be back in football for the new season.

'I turned down a new contract at QPR and offers from two other clubs before the Rovers board approached me. To find a reason why I changed my mind about retiring you have to look back to the last time I was here.

'This club and the majority of this board gave me the opportunity to kickstart my career as a manager and now I've got the chance to help them out. Sometimes you don't get that opportunity.

'There is no doubt in my mind that Bristol Rovers was a great stepping stone for me in my career and I am quite a loyal person. Hopefully I can now pay back some of the help I had when I was first starting out.'

His first game in charge was a pre-season friendly at Mangotsfield, a game that drew a crowd of 1,130 to Cossham Street. Three new players, who all later signed for the club, played a part in the game, namely Scott Howie, Ross Weare and Alvin Bubb.

Weare and Bubb, pictured here with Francis, were with him at QPR and became his first signings. Goalkeeper Howie, who had been between the posts for Reading when Rovers recorded a 6-0 win at the Madejski Stadium in January 1999, eventually joined the club at the end of July after appearing in all of the pre-season games.

One more player, defender Rik Lopez, signed a short term deal before the new season kicked off with a 1-0 win against Torquay United on 11th August.

A game on 9/11

The second coming of Gerry Francis as manager couldn't have got off to a better start.

Fireworks greeted the team as they ran out at the Memorial Stadium for their first home game.

A crowd of 10,127 saw Steve Foster's goal give the side a 1-0 win in that game, against Torquay United, while Ross Weare's only ever league goal helped them to a 2-1 win at Scunthorpe one week later.

There was a single goal win against Wycombe Wanderers in the First Round of the Worthington Cup and, after victory by the same score in the league game against Luton on 25th August, Rovers were top of the Third Division table with a 100% record after three games.

It didn't last and by the time Birmingham City visited the Memorial Stadium for a Second Round Worthington Cup Tie on September 11th, the side had slipped to tenth place in the league.

That September date, of course, is remembered for events that were happening in New York and Washington, and not for a football match in Bristol. All day long horrific footage of the terrorist atrocities in America had unfolded on our television screens but those images had to be put to the back of the mind once the game kicked off.

The sides had already met in a pre-season friendly at the Mem in July, when Rovers had won 2-1.

On this occasion, though, the First Division outfit were far too strong for Rovers and recorded a convincing victory to ease through to the Third Round of the competition by virtue of a 3-0 win.

Andrew Johnson opened the scoring for the visitors just before half time when he met Martin Grainger's free kick and headed past Scott Howie.

The second goal arrived just after the hour mark when Michael Johnson applied the finishing touch from close range after Nicky Eaden had threaded the ball through a ruck of players.

Birmingham wrapped things up on 68 minutes when Danny Sonner picked out Bryan Hughes who beat Howie from 15 yards.

Although they registered nine off target attempts in the 90 minutes, Rovers only managed two on target, one of which was a header from Weare which was well saved by Kevin Poole. The other, a weak header from Andy Thomson, caused the goalkeeper no problems at all.

Pictured here is second half substitute Martin Cameron, who was beginning his second season with the club following his arrival from Alloa Athletic in the summer of 2000.

He was to score six goals in 39 league games for Rovers before returning to Scotland where he turned out for Partick Thistle, St Mirren and Gretna. There were five games for Shamrock Rovers before a final Scottish (Highland?) fling with Forfar Athletic.

Rovers: Howie, Wilson, Foran, Foster, Thomson, Jones, Gall, Mauge, Hillier (Hammond), Ellington, Weare (Cameron)

Substitutes: Trought, Hogg, Clarke

Four Goals Shared

A Memorial Stadium crowd of 6,933 turned up for the game against York City on September 22nd 2001 hoping to see Rovers register their third successive victory following a 1-0 win at Lincoln City and a 2-1 home win against Southend United.

However, they had to be content with a 2-2 draw against the Minstermen.

A scrappy first half ended goalless though Rovers created the best opportunity through Kevin Gall, who saw his effort pushed away by goalkeeper Alan Fettis.

Nathan Ellington had the ball in the York net on 57 minutes, but his effort was ruled out for offside, and Rovers had to wait another 11 minutes before opening the scoring.

Andy Thomson played the ball to Martin Cameron, who curled a left foot shot over the goalkeeper's head from an acute angle, into the far corner of the net, to register his first goal of the season.

They held the lead for just six minutes before the visitors equalised when Graham Potter beat Scott Howie with a free kick while Rovers were still organising their defensive wall.

The lead was regained in somewhat fortuitous circumstances with six minutes of the game remaining as Potter scored at the wrong end of the pitch when he diverted Ellington's cross past his own keeper.

However, the visitors levelled the scores again in the final minute of normal time when the usually reliable Steve Foster failed to clear a ball into the box and it fell kindly to Richard Cooper, who rifled a shot past Howie.

Pictured here during the game are Gall and Potter (currently manager of Premier League side Chelsea). Gall began his career with Cardiff City before moving to Newcastle United who had to pay the Welsh club a considerable sum of money by way of compensation for persuading him to move to the north east.

The Merthyr Tydfil born striker was only 15 at the time of the move and during his time with the Magpies he failed to make a first team appearance.

In March 2001 he joined Rovers on a short term contract until the end of the season, and signed a permanent deal in the summer of that year.

He made a goalscoring debut for Rovers, on 31st March 2001, in a ten minute cameo appearance as a substitute against Stoke City at the Britannia Stadium, but it was only a consolation strike as his side lost 4-1 on the day.

There were to be just five goals in a half century of league games for Rovers before a move to Yeovil Town in 2003. Once he left the Somerset based club he embarked on a nomadic tour of clubs that took in Carlisle, Darlington (twice), Lincoln City, Port Vale, York City, Wrexham, FC Dallas, Workington, Guiseley and Stockport Sports, winning eight Welsh U-21 caps along the way.

Rovers: Howie, Wilson, Thomson, Foster, Foran, Lopez (Trought), Gall, Mauge, Hillier (Pritchard), Cameron, Ellington (Hammond).

Substitutes: Bubb, Clarke.

Through After A Penalty Shootout

On October 31st 2001 Rovers took on Yeovil Town in a Second Round LDV Vans Trophy tie at the Memorial Stadium.

The Glovers were a Conference side at the time, but Rovers only managed to edge them out after a penalty shootout.

The game came at the end of a month in which Rovers had failed to win a league game. Indeed, you had to go back to September 15th for the last one, a 1-0 victory against Lincoln City at Sincil Bank.

The tie game came just three days after a 2-1 home defeat at the hands of another west country side, Plymouth Argyle, and it would be fair to say that it didn't capture the imagination of the fans, as only 4,301 turned up and over 1,000 of them were from Yeovil.

Michael McIndoe gave the visitors a first half lead when, in the 27th minute, he saw his speculative cross deceive everyone and enter the net off the inside of the upright.

It was a lead they held until the 67th minute when striker Alvin Bubb was brought down by goalkeeper Chris Weale and Martin Cameron hammered the resulting penalty high into the roof of the net.

No further goals meant a 30 minute period of extra time but, as there were no further goals, the game went to a penalty shootout.

Rovers converted all five of their spot kicks and Yeovil their first four. Thankfully, McIndoe blasted his penalty over the bar and, by virtue of winning 5-4, Gerry Francis' side went through to the next round of the competition.

The first half performance wasn't good, and half time substitute Bubb was the local newspaper's Man of the Match.

In fact, manager Francis labelled the opening 45 minute performance by his side as unacceptable, saying; *'We lacked passion and desire and we got nervy, which was totally unacceptable.*

'A lot of words were said at half time. I changed some of the personnel and we were much better. As for the penalties at the end, that doesn't do your grey hairs or ticker any good and I was getting quite heated on the sidelines.'

There are a few names in that lineup that many of you will, I'm sure, have forgotten, Bubb most likely being one of them. The diminutive striker had played under Francis at QPR and was signed by his former boss in the summer of 2001. His one season at the Memorial Stadium yielded just 13 appearances.

Neil Ross (pictured) had joined the club on loan, from Stockport County, and appeared in five games before returning to the north west. He later played for Macclesfield Town before embarking on a 'tour' of non league clubs in the Yorkshire/Derbyshire areas.

A spell as manager of Leeds United women was followed by time spent as a coach and manager at Farsley Celtic, though he was sacked by them in January 2022.

Rovers: Howie, Wilson, Thomson, Foster, Foran (Walters), Jones, Gall (Bubb), Mauge (Bryant), Plummer, Cameron, Ross.

Substitutes: Trought, Clarke

Shots Despatched

Rovers' dismal run of league results continued throughout November, another month when they failed to win a league game.

In the FA Cup a goalless draw against Aldershot, at the Recreation Ground, on 17th of the month meant that the non-league side travelled to the Memorial Stadium for the replay ten days later.

By that time Rovers were down in 20th position in League Two and there were real fears for their league safety.

The cup tie, therefore, brought a welcome relief from a hugely disappointing league campaign and a single goal win against lower league opposition was welcomed, even though they were expected to win by a bigger margin.

In the end they were fortunate to go through to the Second Round of the competition as Aldershot gave them a number of scares during a nervous performance in front of a crowd of 4,848.

The only goal of the game arrived six minutes from time and 676 minutes since Rovers had last scored.

The goalscorer was Latvian international Vitalijs Astafjevs who picked up a through ball from Nathan Ellington and drilled a 20 yard shot past visiting goalkeeper Gareth Howells.

After the game, a relieved Gerry Francis said; *'Our goal was a slight miskick but, knowing our luck, had Vitalijs struck it cleanly it would have gone like a bullet straight into the keeper's arms!*

'It was a tight game, with chances at both ends. But the boys deserved something because they hadn't had the best of luck in some of our recent games when they deserved better results for their performances.

'Scott Howie made some good saves for us again. I only had four weeks to find us a keeper when I arrived at the club and got him on a free transfer, but he's come through for us in the last couple of games in particular.'

Howie (pictured) was, indeed, an excellent signing for the club and in two years he was an ever present though he did relinquish his place at half time in the final game of the following season, allowing Ryan Clarke to make his league debut.

The shot stopper was also quite an intelligent man, having studied for, and obtained, a Business Studies degree whilst playing part time for Scottish club Clyde.

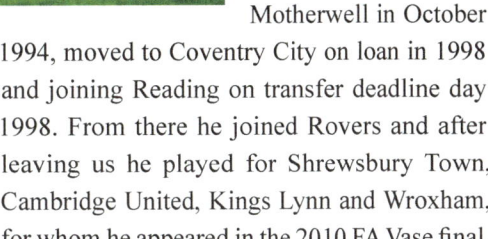

He had won the first of five Scottish U-21 caps before moving to Norwich City in August 1993 and he was on the bench for the Canaries' memorable run in the UEFA Cup in his first season at Carrow Road.

He signed for Motherwell in October 1994, moved to Coventry City on loan in 1998 and joining Reading on transfer deadline day 1998. From there he joined Rovers and after leaving us he played for Shrewsbury Town, Cambridge United, Kings Lynn and Wroxham, for whom he appeared in the 2010 FA Vase final.

Rovers: Howie, Smith, Thomson, Foster, Trought, Challis, Plummer, Mauge, Hillier (Astafjevs), Ellington, Weare (Cameron).

Substitutes: Wilson, Gall, Clarke

The Game That Never Was

Pictured in action against Hartlepool United on December 15th 2001 is Nathan Ellington, and it's a rare photo from a game that lasted all of 12 minutes before being called off.

Garry Thompson had been placed in temporary charge of team affairs as Gerry Francis had taken time off because of serious illness to close family members.

The visitors to the Memorial Stadium that day named former Rovers loanee goalkeeper Anthony Williams and future manager Darrell Clarke in their starting XI while defender Jon Bass, later to become a Rovers player, was on the bench.

Rovers went into the match occupying a bottom four place in Nationwide Division Three with only Torquay United, Carlisle United and Halifax Town below them, while Hartlepool were firmly ensconced in mid table.

The weather in Bristol had been freezing cold and there were doubts as to whether the game would go ahead. Vice Chairman Geoff Dunford was one of those surprised that referee Mark Warren decided that the game could start; *'When I arrived at the ground I saw frost on the pitch and I was very surprised to learn that the game was going ahead. Then, five minutes before the start, we got a message in the boardroom to say that the referee was going to give it ten minutes. But to kick off and abandon it ten minutes later, I find amazing. If the pitch wasn't playable at 3.00pm then it wasn't going to be playable at ten past three.*

'But referees make mistakes during the game, so we shouldn't be surprised if they make mistakes before it.'

He went on to deny that the club had placed any pressure on the Walsall based official to get the game underway; *'We cannot influence the referee in any way. If we could, we wouldn't have got relegated last season.'*

Thompson wasn't happy, either; *'I'm gutted. If you are going to call the game off then you do it beforehand, you don't do it after 12 minutes because when that happens the fans feel as though they have been cheated.*

'If they had known in advance, then at least they could have done something else. All they wanted was to see a game of football. The referee said he was happy with the pitch beforehand, but once the match started, he said players were having trouble standing up and he was going to call it off.

Hartlepool boss Chris Turner agreed with the decision, though; *'It was obvious there were going to be concerns about the pitch. I didn't think it was safe, and you have to think about the players.'*

There were no goals scored in the 12 minutes, and when the game was eventually played, on February 12th 2002, Hartlepool gained a 1-0 win.

This is one of very few photos taken during the 12 minutes of play!

Rovers: Howie, Wilson, Foran, Thomson, Trought, Challis, Hogg, Hillier, Astafjevs, Ellington, Cameron.

Substitutes: Clarke, Ommel, Plummer, Walters, Gall.

Gerry Goes

Manager Gerry Francis missed the first four games of December 2001 on compassionate grounds as close members of his family were seriously ill.

In his absence Garry Thompson once more took over in the hot seat and he was in charge of the game at Swansea on December 21st which Rovers lost 2-1 even though they had taken a third minute lead through Nathan Ellington.

On Christmas Eve Francis, pictured with Director Vernon Stokes and Chairman Geoff Dunford, attended a press conference at the Memorial Stadium to announce his resignation.

He said; 'It is with much regret that due to immediate family illness, I am leaving my position as Manager and Director of Football at Bristol Rovers Football Club.

'The club has been very supportive and given me time off in the hope that my position would improve but, unfortunately, my problems have become long term.

'Football management is a 24 hour, seven day a week job and due to my circumstances this simply has not been possible. Following a discussion with the Board of Directors, we agreed that it would be in the best interests of the club and my family for me to leave.

'Although I have only been at the club for six months, it has been a very difficult job and financially there has been little scope for change. The team had a great start to the season over the first 10 games, before a terrible run of injuries to key players, which affected our results.

'With Nathan Ellington now back to full fitness, results have improved, and we have two important cup games to look forward to in the Leyland DAF Trophy regional semi-final against Bristol City and the FA Cup Third Round tie against Derby County.

'I am also confident that our league results will improve and that the club, for whom I have great affection, will turn the corner, both on and off the field.

'I would like to thank the Directors, players, and all the staff at the stadium, the administrative and commercial team and all the backroom staff, with a special note of thanks to Garry Thompson and Gary Penrice and everyone else connected with the club for their effort, help and support.

'Last, but by no means least, I would like to express my thanks to the supporters of Bristol Rovers for their continued support of the club and their kind thoughts for my family at this difficult time.'

On behalf of the Board of Directors, Geoff Dunford said; 'We all feel for Gerry. He came here to do a job for us, but his personal situation made it impossible for him to carry on. Our thoughts and good wishes are with him and his family.'

As a parting shot, Gerry lent his support to his assistant, Thompson, who was asked to continue in a temporary capacity; 'He knows the club, he knows the players and I think the club would be in good hands, but it's not my decision.'

A Christmas Cracker

Two days after the resignation of Gerry Francis, Rovers took on Leyton Orient at the Memorial Stadium and treated a Boxing Day crowd of 7,458 to a goal feast as they won 5-3.

Garry Thompson, still caretaker manager at this stage, saw Nathan Ellington score the first hat trick of his senior career and said this of his star man afterwards; *'He's going to be something special and some of the things he did out there were magnificent.*

'He still holds on to the ball too long at times, but it takes a special talent to score goals like that and he is looking back to his best again.'

Ellington, pictured during the match, set Rovers on the way to their first three point haul in 15 games when he opened the scoring on 25 minutes. He outpaced Orient's Matthew Joseph before beating goalkeeper Scott Barrett with a left foot shot.

Three minutes later he picked up a pass from Vitalijs Astafjevs inside his own half and set off towards goal before beating Barrett with a shot from the edge of the area.

Two minutes into the second half 'The Duke' turned provider, back heeling a pass into the path of Astafjevs and his low shot beat the visitors' goalkeeper for the third goal of the afternoon.

Steve Watts pulled a goal back for Orient before Ellington completed his hat trick with 73 minutes on the clock, this time scoring with a spectacular 30 yard effort.

Wayne Gray beat Scott Howie to reduce the deficit two minutes later, but Sergio Ommel restored Rovers' two goal advantage in the 89th minute with a header from David Hillier's cross, only for Gray to score his second goal of the afternoon shortly afterwards.

Thompson, as well as praising Ellington, also had nothing but good to say about Lewis Hogg in his first start as skipper; *'Lewis gave a captain's performance and led by example. He was a giant for us and was everywhere.'*

When quizzed about the managerial vacancy, Thompson said he still didn't know if he was taking over from Gerry Francis on a permanent basis; *'It's not about me, it's about getting some stability at the club and the players knowing who is in charge and what is going to be happening. Whoever takes over, whether it's me or someone else, everyone needs to get behind them, but we all need to know who it is going to be so we can get going.*

'I'm not trying to hold a gun to anyone's head, but it needs a decision because the situation with Gerry meant everyone was hanging on for a few weeks. 'There's no real gaffer at the moment and that has an effect and creates uncertainty.'

By the time of the next home game, on December 29th, Thompson had been handed the job on a permanent basis!

Rovers: Howie, Smith, Foran, Wilson, Trought (Jones), Hogg, Hillier, Astafjevs, Gall (Walters), Ommel, Ellington.

Substitutes: Plummer, Cameron, Clarke.

Garry Takes Over

Garry Thompson, pictured here with Chairman Geoff Dunford and Director Ron Craig, was handed a second opportunity to manage Bristol Rovers following the Boxing Day win over Orient.

He had been overlooked for the job the previous summer, after his first stint as caretaker boss, as the Directors elected to bring Gerry Francis back to manage the club for a second time.

Although disappointed then, 'Tommo' had comfortably adapted to the role of assistant manager and was more than ready to take over again, saying; 'Initially I was disappointed not to have been offered the job last summer, but I could see exactly why the club appointed Gerry. He had a wealth of managerial experience and had won promotion for the club in his first spell here, so it was a logical step to bring in someone with his experience and I have to say that I learned an awful lot from him.'

He had his own ideas on how he wanted things done; 'Generally, the players know that I'm quite an easy going person and they can have a laugh and a joke. However, when we are training and preparing for games, I expect everyone to work hard.

'People pay good money to come to watch us play and the least they can expect is to see a Rovers team working their hearts out, having a go and trying to play good football.

'Those are the principles we will always work to, and we'll try to keep building on that. We'll never be the finished article, because no matter how good we become I'm always going to want more.

'As soon as we start training, or when we arrive at the stadium on a matchday, we are going to work and that's something I want to instil into the players. They must also realise that, when they are out on the pitch, they are representing Bristol Rovers.

'Throughout the club we must have players who are responsible and who can portray a good image of the club and of a group of players who work together, keep together as a unit, and care for each other.'

He had spoken to a lot of people about taking the job.

'I contacted Gordon Milne and Dave Sexton, who I knew from my time as a player with Coventry and I also spoke to Ian Atkins, which might surprise some people, as it had been rumoured that I was going to join him at Oxford!

'Essentially, they all said the same thing, in that there are a lot of people who never get the opportunity to manage a football club. They were all surprised that I was even asking for their opinion. I knew what I wanted to do, but I like to get everything right in my mind and it's always good to talk to other people when you have to make an important decision.'

His first game as permanent manager, on December 29th 2001, saw his side beat Darlington 1-0 at the Memorial Stadium.

Pride of Bristol!

After a poor first half of the season Rovers found themselves languishing in 19th place when they travelled to Pride Park, home of Premiership outfit Derby County, for an FA Cup Third Round tie on January 6th 2002.

No one gave them too much hope of progressing, but the game provided the major highlight of a dismal, and depressing, season.

Nathan Ellington's hat trick earned his side a 3-1 win in front of a crowd of 18,549, in what was the shock result of the round. It was the first time a club from the league's basement division had beaten a Premiership side on their own ground.

The home side boasted the likes of Fabrizio Ravanelli and Benito Carbone in their starting lineup but reputations counted for nothing as Rovers, roared on by over 6,000 of their own fans, took the game to their more illustrious opponents.

While Ellington, pictured in action at Pride Park, quite rightly earned all the plaudits it was by no means a one man show as the striker was ably supported by his team mates.

It took Garry Thompson's side just 14 minutes to open their account. The home defenders took far too long to deal with Scott Howie's long clearance and Horacio Carbonari decided to let the ball run through to goalkeeper Mart Poom.

It never reached the custodian, though, as Ellington was first to react and gratefully accepted the opportunity to head over the stranded keeper and into an empty net.

The home side seldom troubled Howie in Rovers goal after the shock of conceding, though the keeper did make a couple of routine saves from Paul Boertien and Adam Bolder.

Five minutes before the break Ellington struck again. The striker eased past Francois Grenet before hitting a shot that took a deflection off Youl Mawene. Although Poom managed to get a hand to the shot he only succeeded in diverting the ball into his own net.

Ellington completed his hat trick on 61 minutes when he controlled a cross from David Hillier on his chest, swivelled and hit a volley that flew past Poom.

Derby did manage a consolation goal two minutes from time when Ravanelli headed in from Carbone's cross. However, the muted celebrations, by players and fans alike, showed that it was too little, too late.

Afterwards, Ellington revealed that he almost didn't get to keep the match ball: *'The referee said he wanted to check on who was being credited with our second goal before he would hand it over!'*

Thompson's post match comments focussed on Ellington's third goal of the afternoon: *'That one was a bit special. He has a special talent. He is strong and raw, and he has a great future. You've seen what he can do against Premiership opposition and he can go a long way in the game.'*

Rovers: Howie, Smith, Foran, Wilson, Challis, Hogg, Hillier, Plummer, Gall (Walters), Ellington, Ommel.

Substitutes: Jones, Cameron, Bubb, Clarke

Sergio, Mark And Che

Pictured surrounding Fabrizio Ravanelli at Pride Park are (from the left) Sergio Ommel, Mark Foran and Che Wilson.

Ommel, a striker, signed for Rovers in November 2001 having previously played in Holland and Iceland.

His made his Rovers debut against Hull City and scored his first senior goal for the club in a 4-1 win against Dagenham & Redbridge in an LDV Vans Trophy tie.

He was popular with supporters during his one season stay, which yielded 10 goals in 28 games in all competitions and appeared to enjoy his time with us.

'I've been made to feel really welcome here, by players and staff alike,' he said, *'I think the standard of football here compares favourably with that in Holland. The main difference is that in Holland the game is more positional, and not as physical as in this country.'*

He returned to Holland after his release, where he continued playing local football.

Central defender Foran started out as a trainee at Millwall before joining Sheffield United. Loan moves to Rotherham and Wycombe Wanderers followed before a permanent move to Peterborough, who matched the £30,000 fee that the Blades had paid Millwall to secure his signature.

There were loan moves to Lincoln City and Oldham Athletic before Crewe Alexandra paid £45,000 to take him to Gresty Road. By the time he arrived at the Memorial Stadium his value had risen to £75,000!

A regular in the first half of the 2000/01 campaign, he then found himself out of favour and only returned for the final two games, by which time Rovers had already been relegated.

The highlight of his Rovers career was, undoubtedly, the FA Cup tie against the Rams;

'It was absolutely unbelievable. It was a brilliant result and there was a fantastic atmosphere inside the ground. The lads played really well and with passion against a Premiership side and it was just a brilliant game to be involved in.'

Wilson, like Foran, was a member of the squad relegated to the basement division in 2000/01.

A right back, he was a trainee at Norwich and made 25 league appearances for them before joining Rovers on a free transfer in July 2000.

A dependable and reliable defender, he stayed for two years, appearing in 75 league games and was settled at the club, and in the area, before being one of several players released in the summer of 2002.

He was amazed at the turnout for the first home game following relegation, and said; *'Our fans have been absolutely magnificent and to get over 10,000 here for our first game after being relegated was brilliant.'*

He later played for Cambridge United, Southend United, for whom he appeared in over 100 games and had loan spells at Brentford and Rotherham. An Achilles tendon injury ended his career prematurely and having completed an undergraduate degree he completed a Masters Degree at Loughborough University in 2014 and, is now working as Head of Football at the University of Bath.

The Late, Late, Show

Following the FA Cup win against Derby County at Pride Park, Rovers crashed out of the LDV Vans Trophy, losing 3-0 against Bristol City at Ashton Gate.

That was followed by a draw against Scunthorpe United at the Memorial Stadium and victory at Gay Meadow, against Shrewsbury Town on January 15th 2002.

Prior to that game manager Garry Thompson had hoped to bring in a loan signing to boost his injury hit squad. Che Wilson, Andy Thomson, Steve Foster, Vitalijs Astafjevs and Drew Shore were all ruled out.

'Tommo' failed in his attempt to bring in a new face, but it made no difference as his side took all three points thanks to a late, late, goal from Sergio Ommel who is pictured signing autographs for Rovers supporters.

It was a scrappy game, played out in front of a crowd of 3,475 and Rovers seldom threatened the home goal in the opening period. However, the Shrews were almost as bad and their best chance came from Luke Rodgers, at the end of the half, whose shot from ten yards hit the inside of the post and came back into play.

Rodgers was fortunate to be playing, as just days earlier he had been arrested in the Hartlepool car park following an alleged fracas with Pool defender Chris Westwood.

The second half followed a similar pattern but just when it seemed as though he game would end goalless, it burst into life. Sam Aiston, who had been cautioned after only two minutes, received a second yellow card in the 90th minute, but there was still time for Rovers to plunder a winner.

Dwayne Plummer's cross was met by Ommel and he forced the ball home from point blank range to give Rovers their third away win of the campaign.

Immediately after the game Thomson told reporters that he was planning talks with Ommel's agent with a view to extending his one month loan with the club, and that he hoped to keep the former Groningen striker until the end of the season.

'Hopefully, it shouldn't be a problem; he likes it here and wants to stay and he has his nose in front of the people waiting in the wings.'

As for the late winner, his fourth goal for Rovers, Ommel said; *'I don't care whether we score in the first minute or the 89th as long as one goes in for us.*

'I thought we defended very well and although Shrewsbury probably had the better of the first half, we came back into it after the break and did create a few chances.

'There wasn't much to choose between the sides, but we limited them to relatively few opportunities and got our reward at the end, so I'm delighted.

'Some might say it was highway robbery, but that doesn't bother me at all.'

Rovers: Howie, Smith, Foran, Jones, Challis, Hogg, Hillier, Plummer, Gall (Walters), Ommel (Cameron), Ellington.

Substitutes: Lopez (R), Trought, Clarke

Swans Savaged

A 2-1 defeat against Torquay United, at Plainmoor on January 19th 2002, was the first time Garry Thompson had suffered defeat following his permanent appointment as manager.

Three days later his side bounced back in style, recording a 4-1 win against Swansea City in front of a Memorial Stadium crowd of 5,725.

On the day of the game it was reported that Charlton Athletic were leading the race to sign Rovers striker Nathan Ellington and it was known that Addicks boss Alan Curbishley had already watched the 20 year old striker in action.

The game against Swansea only served to heighten the interest in Ellington, as he scored his third hat trick in eight games in a Rovers win that saw them move up to 14th place in the table.

Playing under the Memorial Stadium's new floodlights for the first time, Ellington bagged his first goal of the evening from the penalty spot, just before half time. When he forced his way into the area, he was brought down by Swans defender Krystian O'Leary. Referee Mike Dean immediately pointed to the spot and Ellington sent goalkeeper Roger Freestone the wrong way with his effort from 12 yards.

That was in the 43rd minute, and there was still time for another first half Rovers goal. That came from Sergio Ommel who took advantage of hesitation in the Swansea defence when David Hillier floated a free kick into the box and struck a fierce shot past Freestone to give Rovers a two goal cushion going into the half time break.

Ellington was on target again eight minutes into the second half when he took a pass from Trevor Challis and hit a stunning 25 yard effort that went in off the inside of a post.

The visitors did manage to pull a goal back just after the hour mark when Jonathan Coates sent Steve Watkin away and he beat Scott Howie from just inside the box to register his seventh goal of the season.

Four minutes from time Ellington, pictured being closely marked in the game, completed his hat trick when he headed past Freestone from a Vitalijs Astafjevs cross.

Swansea finished in 20th place in League Two that season, three places higher than Rovers. Since then, of course, they have played in the Premier League, though they are currently plying their trade in the Championship.

Manager Thompson was full of praise for Ellington after the match; *'Some of his football was superb. The kid is great because he just wants to play football and score goals and that's what he lives for. I'm happy to talk about the way Nathan plays, his goals and what a lovely kid he is and that's it, because he's our player. We all love him, he wants to be with us, and I want to keep him as long as we can.'*

Rovers: Howie, Smith, Foran, Thomson, Challis, Hogg (Walters), Hillier, Plummer, Astafjevs, Ommel (Cameron), Ellington

Substitutes: Mauge, McKeever, Clarke

Ellington On Target Again

Two days before the visit of Halifax Town to the Memorial Stadium, two of Rovers' long term injury victims, Jamie Shore and Ross Weare, both played 45 minutes of a reserve team game at Luton as they battled to return to full fitness.

Sadly neither of them quite managed it and, eventually, both were forced to retire from the game. That game at Luton also saw AFC Sudbury striker Sam Banya feature for the club after scoring 40 goals in 28 games. Not sure what happened to him!

Manager Garry Thompson, meanwhile, was still fending off interest in Nathan Ellington, with Millwall allegedly the latest in a long line of clubs wanting to take him off our hands!

The league's bottom club, Halifax, duly arrived at the Memorial Stadium on February 9th and went home having suffered a 2-0 defeat as Sergio Ommel and Ellington scored the goals that cheered a crowd of 6,921.

Ommel benefited from a mishit shot from Ellington to open the scoring after 39 minutes. The ball arrived at the Dutchman's feet and he comfortably scored from close range.

Ellington's goal arrived on 70 minutes when he picked up a through ball from Scott Jones, raced past defender Chris Clarke and fired past goalkeeper Barry Richardson from 18 yards.

He almost scored again seven minutes later, when his shot struck the angle of post and crossbar and rebounded to safety.

However, that would have served only to mask what was a truly awful game if the press reports are anything to go by. At the end of the season, Halifax were bottom of the league and were relegated. Thankfully for Rovers, who finished the season one place better off, only one side went down that season.

Afterwards Thompson revealed that Ellington, pictured in action in that game, had almost been substituted before his goal. He had received a hefty knock on the ankle in a challenge from Halifax skipper Graham Richardson, and the manager had substitute Kevin Gall on the sidelines waiting to replace him.

'Nathan lost all feeling in his ankle immediately after the knock and Mark Smith signalled to me that we would need to make a change. I was about to put Kevin on when Nathan made a run that suggested that he might be OK.

'I thought I would give him a minute, then another minute, and soon he looked fine again.'

Dutch striker Ommel, meanwhile, was keen to praise his strike partner; 'He makes space for me and makes it easier for me. I hadn't played a lot of games before coming here, but I think I have picked it up now. I think he always takes a couple of defenders with him.

'I can help him by heading the balls down, which he is always watching for. He can make something out of nothing.'

Rovers: Howie, Wilson, Foran, Thomson, Smith (Plummer), Jones, Hillier, Hogg, Astafjevs, Ellington, Ommel

Substitutes: Mauge, Gall, Greaves, McKeever

Six in a Row

Cheltenham Town were the visitors to the Memorial Stadium on March 6th 2002 and the day before that manager Garry Thompson had unveiled his new assistant, none other than former Chelsea and Northern Ireland striker Kevin Wilson, pictured here with Thompson.

Also a former Northampton Town manager, Wilson was brought in to fill the void left by the departure of Gary Penrice and joined with the club having lost their previous five games.

With 11 games to go, the new man was looking forward to the challenge of taking on Cheltenham the next day; 'People keep telling me that they have only lost once in their last 20 league games, but I'm determined to make it two losses in 21. Garry and I are both bubbly characters and we want the players to enjoy themselves, to express themselves and have the confidence to get the ball down and play attractive football.'

Unfortunately, the new man didn't get off to a winning start and Rovers lost for the sixth time in succession, being eventually undone by one of their former strikers, Julian Alsop.

The Robins had to come from behind to record their victory, as Rovers had taken the lead in the 43rd minute when Sergio Ommel unleashed a fierce shot from the edge of the area giving future Rovers' goalkeeping coach, Steve Book, no chance of saving.

The visitors equalised on the stroke of half time, though, when the future Rovers striker Richard Walker was on hand to register his first Cheltenham goal, scoring from close range after Scott Howie had parried a Michael Duff header into his path.

Alsop netted what proved to be the winner 20 minutes from time, when he rose above a static Rovers defence to head past Howie from a Lee Williams cross.

The talk after the match was of a lack of fitness in the squad, with manager Thompson saying; 'Kevin (Wilson) took one look at the players and told me he didn't think they were fit enough. He's been here less than a week and he's already saying things I've been banging on about all season. Without base fitness you have nothing, and I had a bit of a row about that with Gerry (Francis) early in the season, because he preferred to concentrate on patterns of play rather than conditioning.

'But there was nothing I could do. I was in a position where I had to go with the manager. We've been trying to squeeze fitness work into them during the season, but it's virtually impossible when games are coming thick and fast.

'You need a good month to build up a basic foundation of fitness and that is a luxury I don't have in March.

'This should have been done properly back in July and August.'

Rovers: Howie, Trought (Gall), Wilson, Smith, Lopez, Hogg, Hillier (Jones), Astafjevs (Walters), Challis, Ellington, Ommel

Substitutes: Clarke, Bubb

Double Debut

Rovers travelled to Home Park, Plymouth, on March 30th 2002 when two recent signings, Wayne Carlisle and Ciaran Toner, made their debuts after joining the club on transfer deadline day.

Toner is pictured here in action during the game, being challenged by former Rovers striker Micky Evans. For the second debut boy, Carlisle, it turned out to be an afternoon he will want to forget as he was sent off in the second half. The home side won a close contest 1-0, a result that guaranteed them promotion, while Rovers were left still needing points to ensure they weren't relegated to the Conference.

Garry Thompson's side fell behind to the quickest goal scored that day when Marino Keith found the back of the net after only 29 seconds. The striker was on hand to score from close range after an effort from Steve Adams had rebounded to him off the upright.

Rovers, playing without Nathan Ellington for the first time following his transfer to Wigan Athletic, took a while to settle following the goal, but began to make their mark on the game and the best chance of the opening period fell to James Thomas who shot just wide.

Early in the second half a James Quinn header, from Mark McKeever's corner, hit the underside of the crossbar but that was as close as they came to an equaliser.

The home side also created chances in an open game, the best of which fell to Ian Stonebridge, who saw his shot tipped away by goalkeeper Scott Howie, and future Rovers boss Graham Coughlan, who hit the bar from close range.

Plymouth's task was made easier when Rovers were reduced to ten men. Carlisle, who had been booked in the opening period, picked up a second yellow card on 62 minutes for time wasting which meant his side had to play out the remainder of the game with ten men.

Manager Thompson didn't mince his words in his post-match press conference; *'Some of the referee's decisions were crap, but there again I can't just blame him for us getting beaten. Wayne had already been booked and he showed a little bit of petulance that led to his second card and ultimate dismissal.'*

Toner enjoyed an excellent debut in the middle of the park and imposed himself on proceedings. The Northern Ireland U-21 international had begun his career with Tottenham Hotspur but failed to break into their first team.

He had already spent time on loan with Peterborough before joining Rovers and was to appear in six league games during his brief stay at the Memorial Stadium.

He later played for Leyton Orient, Lincoln City, Cambridge United (loan), Grimsby Town and Rochdale. After leaving Spotland, in 2010, he played non-league football for Harrogate Town and for Guiseley.

Rovers: Howie, Wilson, Foran, Foster, Challis, Carlisle, Toner, Shore, McKeever (Astafjevs), Quinn, Thomas.

Substitiues: Ommel, Walters, Smith, Clarke

Kiddy's Three Red Cards

Two days after complaining about Paul Danson, the referee in charge of the league game at Plymouth, manager Garry Thompson was probably raising a glass or three to another match official, Frazer Stretton, after his side's 2-1 win against Kidderminster Harriers.

Stretton sent off three 'Kiddy' players but, even then, Rovers found it hard to break down a stubborn visitors' defence and only scored the winning goal two minutes from time.

Harriers' caretaker manager Ian Britton, a Gashead and former Rovers youth team player, saw his side go a man down after only four minutes.

As he burst into the box Jamie Thomas, pictured, was brought down by Abdou Sall. The outcome was a red card for the defender and a penalty for Rovers, which James Quinn successfully converted.

In spite being a man down the visitors equalised after 35 minutes when a shot from Ian Foster was parried by goalkeeper Scott Howie into the path of Drewe Broughton and he fired into the net from six yards.

On the stroke of half time the visitors lost their goalkeeper, Gary Montgomery, to the second red card of the afternoon. He had strayed outside his box to clear the ball and his attempt at hacking the ball away rebounded off Sergio Ommel and hit his arm. Referee Stretton gave him his marching orders on the advice of his assistant, Ian Williams.

Rovers failed to make the most of their numerical superiority after the break, much to the frustration of the crowd of 5,711. Just when it seemed as though they would have to settle for a point, though, Ommel was on hand to force the ball over the line after stand in goalkeeper John Danby failed to hold a corner kick taken by Vitalijs Astafjevs.

There was still time for a third red card as well because Ian Foster claimed, rather too forcefully, that the keeper had been impeded.

Incidentally, three interested observers in the Kidderminster side that day were Craig Hinton, Danny Williams and Bo Henriksen, all future Rovers players.

Thompson wasn't to know it, but it was his last home game as Rovers manager. A 2-0 defeat at Field Mill, Mansfield, five days later, was the final straw and his departure was announced a shortly after that.

It must have come as quite a shock to the amiable Brummie, as he had already started to plan for the following campaign.

Just a day after the win against Kidderminster that had banished all fears of relegation, he sent a reserve side out to play Cardiff that included Mangotsfield striker Darren Edwards, Chelsea central defender Pat Baldwin, who was to play, on loan, for Rovers in 2009 and Sunderland defender Steve Harrison. Cardiff won the game 3-0 and Rovers defender Mike Trought was sent off.

Rovers: Howie, Lopez (Walters), Wilson, Foran, Challis, Carlisle, Toner, Shore, McKeever (Astafjevs), Quinn (Ommel), Thomas

Substitutes: Trought, Clarke

Phil Takes Charge For Final Three

Garry Thompson's second spell in the managerial hot seat ended with just three games of the 2001/02 campaign left.

He learnt his fate on April 9th 2002, following a run of results that had seen the club drop to third from bottom of the third division.

While former Rovers player Ray Graydon was immediately installed as favourite to replace Thompson, Director of Youth Phil Bater was handed the task of seeing the side through to the end of the season.

His first game in charge, against Hull City, was the last home match of the season and with Graydon watching proceedings the match ended in a 1-1 draw. Graydon had a watching brief again a few days later when Rovers crashed to a 3-0 defeat at York and was also in the stand at Spotland, home of Rochdale, for the final game of the season on 20th April.

The photo here shows a suited Bater in the Spotland dugout and it was a game in which he handed debuts to Ryan Clarke and Neil Arndale and included youngsters Rob Scott, Drew Shore and David Gilroy in his squad.

A crowd of 5,292 saw an entertaining match, won in controversial circumstances by the home side. Ironically, Rovers turned in one of their best performances in a long while and took a deserved lead just after the half hour mark when James Thomas headed home a cross from Wayne Carlisle.

They held that lead at the half time interval but conceded an equaliser on 63 minutes when Paul Simpson rifled in a close range effort following Matt Doughty's cross. Goalkeeper Scott Howie saved his side from going behind before being substituted, his ever present record for the season intact, to allow Clarke to make his league debut.

The young shot stopper was involved in the incident that led to the home side's winning goal just five minutes from time and it appeared to arrive courtesy of a shocking decision by referee Mark Cowburn.

As home striker Lee McEvilly bore down on his goal, Clarke came off his line and dived at his feet and appeared to catch the ball before McEvilly tumbled to the ground. However, Mr Cowburn didn't see it that way and, much to the amusement of the home fans and the astonishment of the Rochdale players, he awarded a penalty though he didn't even caution Clarke.

'It definitely wasn't a penalty,' said the youngster afterwards, adding *'I got both hands on the ball and actually caught it and as he kicked it out of my hands the ball spilled out and he went over with it.'*

The drama wasn't over, as Clarke kept out Alan McLoughlin's subsequent spot kick, only for Mr Cowburn to rule that he had strayed from his line and ordered a retake which the Rochdale player successfully converted at the second attempt.

Rovers: Howie (Clarke), Lopez (Arndale), Foster, Trought, Challis, Toner, Carlisle, Astafjevs, McKeever, Quinn, Thomas (Gilroy).

Substitutes: Scott, Shore

Two Players Named Lopez

During the 2001/02 season Rovers had two players on their books called Lopez, Rik and Carlos though the latter had a double barrelled (Sanchez-Lopez) surname.

Rik, pictured below, was the fourth signing made by Gerry Francis; in three years with Queens Park Rangers the left back had failed to make a first team appearance and had spent the 2000/01 campaign playing for Portugese Second Division side Desportivo Fierence.

He made his debut as a second half substitute against Darlington on August 27th 2001, a scrappy game that Rovers lost 0-1.

He said afterwards; *'I've waited a long time to make my debut and I was just glad to be involved with the squad as it's all I've wanted since I've been here. To be honest I would have been happy to get on the pitch for just one minute.'*

He went on to make a total of seven league appearances in a Rovers shirt before his release in March 2002.

Carlos, a right sided midfielder, joined Rovers from the Madrid based side Getafe Club de Futbol. He arrived in Bristol prior to Christmas

2001 with two other Spanish players but returned home without signing for anyone. He returned early in 2002 but faced a long wait for the necessary paperwork to be sorted before he eventually became a Rovers player. The delay was down to Getafe's reluctance to release him, and it wasn't until February 8th that everything was deemed to be in order.

He made his debut against Hartlepool four days later, a game that Rovers lost 1-0 at the Mem. He must have made an impression, as he picked up the sponsor's Man of the Match Award!

It was the first of his six appearances in a Rovers shirt, the final one coming in the last game of the season at Rochdale.

Speaking before his final game, he said; *'I love it here and whatever happens, whether I go or whether I stay, I'll always remember my time here at Bristol Rovers as it's been a fantastic experience for me.'*

His release was confirmed after that game and I believe he returned to Spain.

Ray's Return

Ray Graydon's appointment as Director of Football was confirmed on April 24th 2002 and he admitted it was a challenge he was looking forward to.

'I'm not a miracle worker and this will be a long term thing and anybody who thinks I can win promotion simply by clicking my fingers can forget it.

'I was born in Frenchay, went to school near the old Eastville ground and grew up supporting the club with my Dad, who was in the crowd singing Goodnight Irene when they beat Manchester United in the 1950's.

'Jobs were available at other clubs, but you have a gut feeling when you think something is right, and I love a challenge. If someone says I can't do something, then my first instinct will be to try and prove them wrong. I was a supporter and player at the club and that stays with you, although I never thought I would be coming back here one day as manager.'

The new manager went on to make a number of pertinent comments. For instance, he wanted to reduce the size of the playing squad from 31 to 20, realised there wasn't a huge amount of money available to bring players in and admitted he was something of a disciplinarian, though he refuted the 'sergeant major' tag that some had given him.

He ended with these thoughts: 'The club needs changing, there is major surgery needed and it won't be all comfortable because a few tears will probably be shed.

'I will probably have to put a few noses out of joint and I'm not looking forward to looking people in the eye and telling them there is no contract here for them.

'But I think there is fantastic potential here, although it means nothing unless it is fulfilled. I want to enjoy it as well.'

His first task as manager was to release a number of players, among them Che Wilson, Mark Foran, Sergio Ommel, Jamie Thomas, Mike Trought, Alvin Bubb, Mark Smith, Mark Walters, Carlos Lopez, Steve Foster, David Hillier and Ronnie Mauge. Striker Ross Weare announced his retirement due to injury, and the manager had still to hold contract talks with Wayne Carlisle and Ciaran Toner, while James Quinn was thought to be joining a club in Holland.

Graydon was expected to bring in his former assistant at Walsall, Chris Nicholl, but on this occasion the rumours were unfounded because, on May 7th he brought in John Still.

The two had never worked together before, but Still had vast experience of working in the lower leagues, having been in charge at Barnet, Peterborough, Maidstone, and Dagenham & Redbridge, though not necessarily in that order!

The managerial duo, pictured here, were soon making their mark as the signings of Kevin Austin, Anwar Uddin, Adam Barrett and Danny Boxall were announced shortly after Still's arrival at the Memorial Stadium.

Defeat at Plainmoor

Ray Graydon's first league game in charge was at Torquay United, on August 9th 2002 and he went into the new season having appointed a new captain in Adam Barrett, the former Plymouth Argyle and Mansfield Town defender.

It was a game that ended in defeat, the Seagulls running out 2-1 winners in front of a crowd of 4,937.

Graydon's side included six players who were making their Rovers debut; Barrett, Danny Boxall, Anwar Uddin (who was also making his first ever appearance in the league), Rob Quinn, Paul Tait and Guiliano Grazioli while a seventh new boy, Kevin Austin, missed out through injury.

Quinn, a former Republic of Ireland U-21 international, moved to the Memorial Stadium from Oxford United, having previously played for Crystal Palace and Brentford.

Tait arrived from Crewe Alexandra, and Rovers fought off interest from Port Vale and Mansfield to capture the 27 year old striker whose career began at Everton and who had also played non-league football for Northwich Victoria and Runcorn.

Rovers got off to a dream start when, with only five minutes on the clock, Grazioli curled a shot into the top corner of the net which left home 'keeper Kevin Dearden clawing thin air.

Graydon's side held on to their lead until the final minute of the first half when former Liverpool winger Neil Prince picked up a short corner and delivered a telling cross into the box where Martin Gritton headed past Scott Howie.

It was a disappointing end to a half in which Rovers had played the better football but only had the one goal to show for their efforts.

They continued to force the home side back for long periods of the second half and Boxall went close to adding a second goal but his 25 yard effort thudded against the crossbar and rebounded to safety.

And then came the first of two controversial penalty decisions, one given, one not. The first went to the home side as they were awarded a spot kick when Tony Bedeau went to ground after a Trevor Challis challenge and Alex Russell beat Howie from 12 yards.

Rovers weren't so fortunate with their own claims for a penalty in the final minute of the game when Rueben Hazel sent Grazioli sprawling as he arrived in the Torquay area. Referee Neil Prosser refused to award a penalty and that, as they say, was that!

Graydon refused to criticise the match official afterwards, saying; *'Don't ever ask me about incidents involving referees because I don't comment on them.'*

His Torquay counterpart, Leroy Rosenior, was a little more forthcoming; *'It was one of those days when a couple of decisions went our way and no doubt it will even out over the course of the season.'*

The photo from the game, reproduced here, shows home goalkeeper Dearden reaching the ball before Grazioli.

Rovers: Howie, Boxall, Uddin, Barrett, Challis, Carlisle (Richards), Bryant (Astafjevs), Quinn, McKeever, Tait, Grazioli.

Substitutes: Hogg, Gilroy, Clarke

Away Shirts 2 Home Shirts 1

Rochdale arrived at the Memorial Stadium on August 17th 2002 minus their kit, which was on their kit van stuck in heavy traffic in the Midlands.

Consequently, they had to wear Rovers' away strip of stone and black quarters. It didn't put them off, as the shirts registered a win, but not for the Gas! (Paul Tait is pictured sandwiched between two Rochdale players wearing Rovers away kit)

After a defeat and a draw in their opening two games, Rovers were hoping to register their first win of the new campaign.

Rochdale were the better side in the first half and it came as little surprise when they opened the scoring on 39 minutes. Player manager Paul Simpson was allowed too much time on the ball and he picked out Clive Platt with his ball into the box and he headed past Scott Howie from close range.

Somehow, though, Rovers conjured up an unexpected equaliser right on the stroke of half time. Goalkeeper Neil Edwards could only parry Wayne Carlisle's shot as far as Simon Bryant and he registered his second senior goal for the club when he fired in from close range.

Rovers enjoyed a much better second half but conceded a second goal with just 12 minutes of the game remaining. A poor pass by Lewis Hogg, on as a substitute for Bryant, saw Simpson pick up the loose ball on the edge of the area and curl a superb shot past Howie to give his side all three points.

Ironically, both of Rochdale's goalscorers that afternoon had played for Graydon when he had been in charge at Walsall and the Rovers' boss had sold Platt to Rochdale for £100,000 in 1999.

'I didn't feel that he was quite good enough to play in the First Division,' said Graydon, adding 'I still believe that, but he's got better and at this level he's a good player. I thought he did a good job for them and I'm glad in a way because I spent a lot of time with him on the training ground.'

Simpson had spent a ten game loan spell at Walsall and of him Graydon had this to say: 'Wolves didn't want Paul when I took him because his legs had gone as far as the First Division was concerned. He came to Walsall and showed some real quality and we saw it again here, without him really having to run. But you can't buy experience like that.'

As for his own side, the Rovers' boss said: 'We all want the first win, and nobody more than the players.

'I keep saying we have a group of people who have just been thrown together, but their expectations are higher than anybody else's. They think that because they have had a good pre-season they can come together after five or six weeks and go on and do something.'

Rovers: Howie, Boxall, Uddin, Barrett, Challis, Carlisle, Bryant (Hogg), Quinn, McKeever (Richards), Tait, Grazioli.

Substitutes: Gall, Shore, Clarke

A First For Ray

It wasn't until August 27th 2002 that Ray Graydon was able to celebrate his first win as a Bristol Rovers manager.

It was the club's sixth competitive game of the season and it's fair to say that the natives were becoming restless! Still, a Memorial Stadium crowd of 6,644 saw Rovers beat Swansea City 3-1 thanks to goals from Giuliano Grazioli (pictured), Paul Tait and Vitalijs Astafjevs.

Grazioli opened the scoring in the 32nd minute, pouncing on Tait's flick on from a long clearance by goalkeeper Scott Howie and nodding the ball over the head of visiting custodian Roger Freestone. It was the striker's third goal of the season.

Seven minutes into the second half Tait doubled the advantage after Freestone parried a shot from Astafjevs up in the air. The lanky striker powered a close range header into the net for his first goal in a Rovers shirt.

The visitors pulled a goal back with ten minutes remaining when substitute Dave Moss met a speculative cross from fellow substitute Michael Howard and headed past Howie.

Graydon's side didn't buckle, however, and restored their two goal advantage six minutes later when Astafjevs powered a shot past Freestone to calm any nerves amongst his team mates and the crowd.

Graydon was delighted to see his team get off the mark and said; *'It's a big relief for everyone, because of the expectations here.*

'It's difficult for us to go without a win whether it's for two games, three, four or more. It's great for everyone connected with the club that we have now got this out of the way.'

There were words of praise for two of his goalscorers, Astafjevs and Tait; *'Vitalijs came into the team for the game at Carlisle on Saturday and although he didn't play all that well, I said at half time that we had to get him on the ball more because he can make things happen.*

'He's not the strongest player in the world in terms of grit and digging in, but he has quality and he showed that in this game.'

As for Tait, he said; *'There had been rumblings from the crowd who weren't happy with the way Paul played in his last performance at home and then he missed a penalty at Carlisle in our last game.*

'His record in the past in terms of goals hasn't been good and some people probably wondered why I'd brought him to the club. But I think he has some quality, and I am prepared to work with players that other clubs have turned away if I think I can bring something out of them.

'I thought his performance was fantastic and as well as scoring he set up the first goal for Giuliano.'

Rovers: Howie, Boxall, Uddin, Barrett, Challis, Carlisle, Hogg, Quinn, Astafjevs, Tait, Grazioli (Gall).

Substitutes: McKeever, Bryant, Richards, Clarke

A Costly Penalty Miss

In the build up to the home game against Exeter City on September 14th 2002, Rovers terminated the contract of midfielder Dwayne Plummer for what was described as gross misconduct.

No details were revealed by the club because, it was stated, that the matter was in the hands of solicitors, though manager Ray Graydon did say this; 'When I arrived here everyone told me that Dwayne had talent, although I only had the chance to see a little of it.

'It is sad that I have had to be a part of this decision, but discipline is paramount, whether inside or outside the club.'

Graydon had seen a Rovers reserve side in action during the week and they pulled off a 4-1 win against Northampton as a number of players hoped to force their way into contention for the game against the Grecians.

As it was, the manager made two changes for the game, replacing Mark McKeever with Vitalijs Astafjevs and Lewis Hogg with Simon Bryant.

The visitors took the lead in the 27th minute when Paul Tait was penalised for a foul, though it appeared that he was the victim rather than the culprit. Nevertheless, the resulting free kick was launched into the area and Anwar Uddin failed to clear, under pressure from James Coppinger, who set up Steve Flack with the opportunity to hit a low shot past Scott Howie from 15 yards.

Rovers equalised following a free kick of their own on 38 minutes. Giuliano Grazioli was upended and Wayne Carlisle's free kick into the area saw Tait lose his marker before glancing a header wide of future Rovers goalkeeper Kevin Miller (both pictured).

Graydon's side squandered a golden opportunity to take the lead seven minutes into the second half when they were awarded a penalty when Tait went to ground under a challenge from Miller.

However the Exeter keeper redeemed himself by making an excellent save from Grazioli's spot kick.

There were no further goals and the Rovers fans in a crowd of 6,498 had to be content with a point that moved their side up to 16th in the league standings.

Graydon said that the overriding feeling after the game was one of frustration; 'It seems, at the moment, no matter how much we work with the players and the response we get from them, we just can't get that bit of luck that you need to win games.

'The players are so frustrated. They were crying into their tea in the dressing room afterwards thinking they should have won the game but hadn't done it.

'We have thousands of people who turn out hoping to see us win and the players were saying how much they appreciate what the fans are doing to help the cause. Everybody at the club is feeling frustration at the moment.'

Rovers: Howie, Boxall, Challis, Uddin, Barrett, Bryant (Hogg), Astafjevs, Quinn, Tait, Grazioli (Richards), Carlisle.

Substitutes: McKeever, Warren, Clarke

Rovers Score Five at Shrewsbury

It had taken Rovers six games to register their first win of the season, a 3-1 victory against Swansea, on August 27th 2002.

By then they had bowed out of the League Cup in the first ever preliminary tie to be played in that competition, suffering a home defeat against league new boys Boston United, and ended the month in 19th place.

September proved to be a little better as, following defeat at Macclesfield Town, they had drawn with Exeter City and beaten Bury in games at the Memorial Stadium.

On September 21st Ray Graydon's side travelled to Gay Meadow, the then home of Shrewsbury Town, and took all three points with a 5-2 win with Giuliano Grazioli scoring a hat trick.

The first goal, which gave Rovers a half time lead, came in the 35th minute after home goalkeeper Ian Dunbavin punched away a cross from Paul Tait as far as Grazioli, who headed home from six yards.

Shrewsbury equalised two minutes into the second half when Karl Murray let fly from 25 yards. Although goalkeeper Scott Howie appeared to have the shot covered and got a touch to it. The ball looped up over his head and into the net.

Rovers regained the lead on 53 minutes when Grazioli scored his second goal of the afternoon when he touched home a cross from Astafjevs at the near post.

Three minutes later Astafjevs scored himself. The Latvian lobbed the ball over a defender, moved towards the edge of the area and fired a shot past Dunbavin.

Grazioli completed his hat trick with 65 minutes on the clock, sidefooting the ball home after taking a pass from Astafjevs and is seen here celebrating with Tait. The home side pulled another goal back when a header from Luke Rogers went in off of Anwar Uddin who was credited with an own goal, but Rovers added a fifth ten minutes from time through Wayne Carlisle.

Dunbavin failed to hold a shot from Tait and could only push it into the path of Carlisle who took great delight in firing a shot past the stranded keeper.

Grazioli's three goals had all been scored from close range and he said afterwards: *'I wouldn't mind 30 like that this season. I could hardly miss any of them because I think the furthest of the three was probably only three yards out.'*

Graydon decided not to attend the post-match press conference and sent his assistant, John Still, to speak with the media representatives. He revealed that Grazioli, a player he had signed when manager of Peterborough, had once scored a hat trick for the Posh against Barnet when he was manager there.

'He scored three when Peterborough beat us 9-1, but what he fails to say is that two of them came when we were down to eight men!'

Rovers: Howie, Boxall, Barrett, Uddin, Challis, Quinn, Bryant, Astafjevs (McKeever), Carlisle (Gall), Tait, Grazioli (Hogg).

Substitutes: Clarke, Richards

Defeat at Darlo

Rovers travelled to play Darlington, at their Feethams ground, on October 5th 2002, having suffered a 2-1 home defeat against Kidderminster Harriers the previous week.

They returned home empty handed after a Barry Conlon goal had given the home side all three points. In addition, they finished the game with ten men following Paul Tait's red card in first half stoppage time.

Going into the match Darlington were the team under pressure, having gone seven games without a win, and there was talk that manager Tommy Taylor could be on the way out if things didn't improve.

Conlon's goal arrived after just 19 minutes. Neil Wainwright's cross in from the left saw goalkeeper Scott Howie attempt to punch clear. However, he misjudged the flight of the ball and it fell to Conlon who headed into an unguarded net.

Rovers almost equalised when Giuliano Grazioli saw his shot well saved by former Rovers' custodian Andy Collett, but manager Ray Graydon clearly wasn't pleased with the way his side were performing and with 11 minutes of the half remaining he replaced Simon Bryant with Lewis Hogg.

Graydon's displeasure was intensified moments before the half time whistle when Tait received his red card. When Wayne Carlisle's free kick arrived in the Darlington area referee Mr Kaye awarded the home side a free kick after Tait and Stuart Whitehead went for the ball.

However, the match official then consulted his linesman and showed a red card to the Rovers striker for allegedly aiming a head butt at his opponent.

Rovers did well not to concede again after the break as they were always susceptible to being hit on the counter attack as they pushed men forward in search of an equaliser.

They almost managed it when Vitalijs Astafjevs saw his shot from 12 yards hit the upright before being cleared, though that was the only real chance they created.

Inevitably, the red card incident was high on the agenda when Graydon faced the press afterwards: *'Paul Tait was sent off for putting his head towards one of their players, and if I could take his house away from him, I'd do it.*

'There is a fine structure in place at the club and he'll have all of that and the kitchen sink thrown at him. He is certainly going to be as harshly dealt with as he has ever been in his life. I've made my feelings about disciplinary matters very clear.

'Tait had been the best player on the pitch up until that point. I told him at half time he had become the worst player with one action.

'I feel so strongly about these things that players who do it can leave the club. I'm not bothered about who they are or where they come from.'

The photo shows midfielder Rob Quin in action during the game.

Rovers: Howie, Boxall (Austin), Barrett, Uddin, Challis, Carlisle, Bryant (Hogg), Quinn, Astafjevs, Tait, Grazioli (Richards)

Substitutes: Clarke, McKeever

David's Debut

They weren't to know it, but the point that Rovers picked up in a 2-2 draw against York on October 19th 2002 would be their last in the league until Boxing Day, when they beat Swansea at the Vetch Field.

For this game at Bootham Crescent Ray Graydon handed a debut to Brighton's David Lee, who had arrived at the Memorial Stadium on a month's loan.

Goalkeeper Ryan Clarke, who had made his debut in the 2-0 win against Lincoln seven days earlier, kept his place in the side and he was the first of the two goalkeepers to pick the ball out of the net that afternoon.

Rovers had already lost Trevor Challis and Kevin Austin through injury when the home side were awarded a 39th minute penalty after a ball into the area struck Vitalijs Astafjevs on the arm and Peter Duffield sent Clarke the wrong way with his spot kick.

Rovers then scored twice in four minutes to take a lead into the half time break. Anwar Uddin registered his first ever league goal shortly after York's opener, when he hit a low right foot shot past Alan Fettis and then Astafjevs beat the keeper with a superb shot from outside the area which flew into the top corner of the net.

Astafjevs became the third injury victim of the afternoon when he was stretchered off just after the hour mark, but Graydon's side battled on and looked as though they would return to Bristol with all three points.

Deep into the five minutes of stoppage time, though, the home side conjured up a controversial equaliser. They were awarded a contentious free kick just outside the area for what appeared to be a push by Adam Barrett on Lee Nogan and with Rovers still lining up their defensive wall Stephen Brackstone curled the ball into the net off the inside of a post.

Rovers were furious that the goal was allowed to stand as they were adamant that future Premier League referee Howard Webb had told York not to take the free kick until he blew his whistle, but their complaints were in vain.

Webb's performance in this game was rated as 'mediocre' in the local press!

The David Lee who made his debut in this game is not to be confused with former Chelsea player of the same name, who played for Rovers under Ian Holloway.

This David, pictured in action at York, began his career with Tottenham Hotspur before joining Southend United, in August 2000. From Roots Hall he joined Hull City, and then Brighton & Hove Albion and it was from there that he signed for Rovers.

He left at the end of his loan spell and later played for Thurrock, Oldham, Stevenage and Aldershot. His last known club was Canvey Island, with whom he spent the 2008/09 season.

Rovers: Clarke, Uddin, Barrett, Austin (Bryant), Challis (Boxall), Carlisle, Astafjevs (Richards), Quinn, McKeever, Lee, Grazioli

Substitutes: Gilroy, Howie

A Fifth Consecutive Defeat

Rovers lost a Director and gained a player in the build up to the home game against Southend United on November 9th 2002.

The Director to go was Bob Andrews who decided to resign, after 13 years on the board, because of family and business commitments.

The player was central defender Chris Plummer (pictured watching Adam Barrett attacking the Southend goal), who arrived on loan from Queens Park Rangers having not played a first team game in a year, after breaking his ankle in November 2001.

'Getting back to fitness has taken a while,' said Plummer after signing, 'but I'm fully fit now and see this as a good opportunity to get some first team football under my belt.

Ray Graydon's side had lost their previous four league games and extended it to five after suffering a 0-1 defeat in front of a crowd of 5,691.

The only goal of the game was scored by Tes Bramble, who beat goalkeeper Scott Howie with an angled drive with 78 minutes on the clock. The result left Rovers fourth from bottom just two points clear of the relegation places, but in his post-match press conference Graydon insisted it wasn't a time to panic; 'We are involved at the wrong end of the table and the last thing this club needs right now is a dogfight among the bottom two or three.

'We've lost five on the trot and that's not a statistic I've been associated with in my life before.

'It's not one I want now, but I have to face it and make sure I make the right decisions.

'The easiest way to react when things are going wrong is to start shouting, blaming people and tearing things up. But that's not what I'm about. I'm trying to create something at this football club and I'm still very focused on that.'

As for the game itself, he said; 'I thought that in patches our football was the best that it has been for a while and there was plenty to be pleased about in terms of effort, but we didn't have the goals at the end of it.

'I have been entrenched in the game all my life and know that when things aren't going well you don't get any luck, but I honestly felt we did enough to win.

'The reason we didn't was because we didn't take our chances and made the one mistake that allowed them to score.

'My reaction isn't to go in and start throwing teacups at players because I feel they are doing what they can. But winning games is the nature of the business we are in, and we have to find a way of doing it, and quickly.'

The Southend game was the first of three consecutive home games, none of which were won and Graydon really did have a crisis on his hands!

Rovers: Howie, Boxall, Plummer, Barrett, Bryant, McKeever, Quinn, Hogg, Lee (Carlisle), Coote (Grazioli), Tait.

Substitutes: Shore, Gilroy, Clarke

Diamonds Defeat

Following their FA Cup first round replay win against Runcorn FA Halton, in which Dave Gilroy scored his first senior goal for the club, Rovers travelled to face Rushden & Diamonds in a league fixture on November 30th 2002.

Ray Graydon's side hadn't won in the league since beating Lincoln City at the Memorial Stadium on October 12th and had slipped to 21st in the Third Division table.

Ahead of the game, a Kevin Gall goal had given a Rovers reserve side a 1-0 win against Reading's second string in a game played at Mangotsfield's Cossham Street ground and Graydon had included three triallists in his side for that game, namely Sonny Parker (Birmingham), Kevin Street (Northwich Victoria) and Leon Bell (Barnet).

Parker did eventually sign for the club, while Street was taken on immediately and joined two more new signings in the squad for the Rushden game, Graham Hyde and Bradley Allen.

Nene Park, sadly now demolished, was a comfortable venue with an amazing training complex and hosted a crowd of 3,960 for the game. By the end of the 90 minutes Rovers winless run had been extended and they had dropped another rung in the league standings as the hosts ran out winners by two goals to one.

It was, though, a much improved performance from Graydon's side and they took the lead on 12 minutes when Giuliano Grazioli fired a penalty kick past goalkeeper Billy Turley after Paul Tait had been fouled by Onandi Lowe. (Tait is pictured facing two Diamonds defenders, the one to the left being former Rovers defender Marcus Bignot).

The lead lasted just nine minutes, though, and it was Lowe who put the home side back on level terms when he lashed home a 30 yard free kick which evaded the defensive wall and goalkeeper Scott Howie.

The winning goal arrived in the 72nd minute and was a somewhat scrappy affair. Stuart Gray's corner was touched towards goal by Barry Hunter and in the ensuing scramble Paul Hall managed to force the ball over the line.

Graydon let rip in his post-match press conference; *'If we keep defending as we did today, we will continue to lose games and we've conceded two goals today that we could have done something about.*

'If defenders aren't going to put their foot through the ball then we will lose. There were some improvements, but I am not happy. This was a game we should have taken something from, and they are a side at the top of the table, too.

'We had three new players, but we can't keep saying we need time. We need results now.

'I always try to look for positives and there were some, but this type of story is becoming all too familiar.

'We do a lot of work during the week, we work on our play in training, we bring some new players in, but we are still going back with a loss.'

Rovers: Howie, Boxall, Challis (Bryant), Barrett, Austin, Quinn, Tait, Grazioli (Allen), Hyde, Astafjevs, Street (Gilroy).

Substitutes: Hogg, Clarke

Signing off With a Point

Just a week after they had slumped to the bottom of the table following a 3-1 defeat at Cambridge, Rovers saw out the calendar year 2002 with a home draw against Boston United on December 28th.

Ray Graydon's side had recorded a surprising 1-0 win at Swansea on Boxing Day, but they hadn't won a league game at home since October 12th and in the intervening 10 weeks loan signings Adrian Coote and Chris Plummer had been and gone, while four more players, Bradley Allen, Kevin Street, Graham Hyde and Richard Rose had arrived.

In their first season as a league club, Boston were making their second visit to the Memorial Stadium. They had recorded a 2-0 win in a preliminary round of the League (Worthington) Cup back in August, and probably fancied their chances of leaving Bristol with another win under their belts.

It took just seven minutes for them to get on the scoresheet on this occasion. Simon Weatherstone's ball into the box found Richard Logan who hit a low angled drive past Scott Howie as Rovers defenders hesitated.

The remainder of the half was a fairly scrappy affair and Boston held their lead until the half time whistle.

Graydon made a half time substitution, replacing Allen with Dave Gilroy, and his side played much better in the second period, though it took them until the 85th minute to get back on level terms, courtesy of a Wayne Carlisle penalty.

Vitalijs Astafjevs, was fouled in the area and Carlisle comfortably beat Paul Bastock with his spot kick.

Not for the first time that season, assistant manager John Still was sent to discuss the game with the media representatives after the game.

'When you lose eight games on the bounce, it becomes difficult to believe in what you are doing.

But taking four points from the two Christmas games has given everyone a lift.

'It has proved we are better than our results suggested. The players have always believed that to be the case, but individual errors were costing us.

'We've cut those out in the last two games and that has given us confidence to look forward with optimism. It's now a case of adding to the base we have established and kicking on. If we can pick up where we left off against Boston, I see no reason why we cannot get ourselves *away from the wrong end of the table.'*

Wayne Carlisle, pictured, had been signed for Rovers by Garry Thompson and was sent off on his Rovers debut, down at Plymouth in March 2002.

The holder of nine Northern Ireland U-21 caps, he had played for Crystal Palace and Swindon before arriving at the Memorial Stadium and went on to play for Leyton Orient, Exeter and Torquay. At the time of writing he is assistant manager at Rotherham United.

Rovers: Howie, Boxall, Barrett, Austin, Rose, Carlisle, Quinn, Astafjevs, Street (McKeever), Tait, Allen (Gilroy).

Substitutes: Bryant, Parker, Clarke

A Home Win At Last

Two goals in the last five minutes of a game against Scunthorpe United on January 18th 2003 saw Rovers record their first victory at the Memorial Stadium since early October.

David Gilroy, pictured, set up Vitalijs Astafjevs on 12 minutes but the Latvian's shot hit the crossbar and rebounded to safety.

It was the best chance of a first half that became increasingly scrappy and there were no goals for the crowd of 6,617 to cheer.

Rovers went close again eight minutes after the break when Wayne Carlisle hit a low right foot drive against the post with Scunthorpe keeper Tom Evans well beaten.

The visitors took the lead, against the run of play, with 63 minutes on the clock following a mistake by Kevin Austin. The defender attempted to deal with a hopeful ball played into the area but allowed it to run away from him and Martin Carruthers gratefully accepted the opportunity to hit a shot past Scott Howie to register his 15th goal of the season.

Rovers had to wait until five minutes from time before equalising. Carlisle hit a deep cross from the right which was headed back across the face of goal by Mark McKeever where Astafjevs hit a shot high into the net.

Three minutes later Rovers were ahead when Carlisle unleashed a stunning free kick from 25 yards which flew past Evans and into the net.

Scunthorpe's misery was compounded a minute from time when Wayne Graves was dismissed following his second yellow card.

Carlisle's goal was his third in successive home games, following his penalties against Boston and Torquay and the midfielder revealed the secret behind his success from dead ball situations: 'I used to practice free kicks quite a lot when I was at Crystal Palace, but I've never hit a better one than the one I scored today, nor a more important one, because we really needed the points.'

Graydon was delighted with his side's late rally, saying: 'The players have been working flat out.

'I've said before they've not let us down in terms of fitness, and that was shown by the way they came back at the end of the game. It was a team effort and a fantastic way to finish a match with a goal worthy of winning any game.'

Gilroy was a promising young striker and appeared in 18 league games for Rovers without scoring, though he did register a goal in an FA Cup tie against Runcorn FC Halton in November 2002.

Now a Director of a Bristol Sports marketing company, he played for a number of non-league clubs after leaving the Memorial Stadium, including Bath City, Forest Green Rovers, Clevedon Town, Weston-super-Mare, Chippenham Town, Newport County, Woking and Frome Town.

Rovers: Howie, Boxall, Barrett, Austin, Rose, Carlisle, Quinn, Astafjevs, Street (McKeever), Tait, Gilroy (Allen).

Substitutes: Hogg, Parker, Clarke

Cumbrians in Control

Rovers took on Carlisle United at the Memorial Stadium on February 1st 2003, a week after taking a point from a goalless draw against Boston United.

However, the Cumbrians secured a 2-1 victory that saw Ray Graydon's side slip to the foot of the Division Three table.

Kevin Street is the Rovers player shown here in action during that game.

In the build up to the game it was anticipated that the Share Scheme initiative would pass the £250,000 mark just seven weeks after it had been launched.

The Scheme's new slogan was launched at the game, known as '5-4-3-2- and I'm one of them', which came about as it had been calculated that 5,432 people were needed to sign up if the ambitious target of £3m was to be reached. (It was to pass the £1m mark in October 2013).

Rob Quinn was suspended, so Graydon recalled Graham Hyde, who had recovered from a thigh strain sustained on Boxing Day. However, the manager was without the services of Trevor Challis who was due to have an ankle operation the following week, and Bradley Allen who was missing with a stomach problem.

Graydon had to make another change on the day of the match as on loan defender Richard Rose was ruled out through illness and he was replaced by Anwar Uddin.

Giuliano Grazioli, who had been expected to take a place on the bench, made a surprise return to first team duty at the expense of Dave Gilroy.

It appeared to be a wise move by the manager to include the striker, as he gave Rovers a 33rd minute lead, though he was helped by a defensive error.

A Danny Boxall cross from the right saw Carlisle's Brian Shelley knock the ball across the face of his own goal right into the path of Grazioli who gratefully seized the opportunity to score his 11th goal of the season.

They held the lead until just before half time when Shelley made amends for his earlier error and got down the right before crossing to Craig Farrell who side footed the ball home from ten yards.

Five minutes into the second half the visitors took the lead when Darren Kelly crossed from the right and found the unmarked Richie Foran, who headed in from close range.

That was the end of the scoring, and even though Carlisle's Jon McArthy was red carded on 69 minutes, Graydon's side failed to take advantage and left the pitch to boos and chants of 'what a load of rubbish' from the home fans.

Speaking after the game the manager said; *'I feel as bad as the supporters, and probably a bit worse, because I started supporting this team when I was a kid of five or six.*

'Now it's my job to run it as manager and I have to do everything in my power to make sure we stay in this division.'

Rovers: Howie, Boxall, Barrett, Uddin, Austin, Carlisle, Hyde, Street, Astafjevs (Bryant), Tait (Gilroy), Grazioli.

Substitutes: Hogg, Parker, Clarke

A Long Awaited Win

Rovers headed into their away game at Bury on March 4th 2003 without a win since January 18th some six games beforehand.

They had managed to keep a point above bottom side Exeter City and had played out a goalless draw with their Devon hosts the previous Saturday, but there was a real concern that Conference football beckoned.

Ray Graydon's side took all three points on this occasion, though, as Rob Quinn's second half goal was enough to record a win at Gigg Lane and move the club up to 20th in the league standings.

The manager made two changes to his starting lineup for the game, recalling skipper Adam Barrett after his one match suspension, in place of Sonny Parker, while Kevin Street replaced the injured Chris Llewellyn.

As he had done at Exeter, Graydon called on a Rovers supporter to join a pre match huddle out on the pitch and on this occasion it was 12 year old James Burke, whose father, also named James, had been invited on to the St James' Park pitch.

First half chances were few and far between, but Rovers gave a reasonable account of themselves and deserved to be on level terms at the break.

On 65 minutes, though, Graydon's side took the lead. The goal came when Graham Hyde picked out Street down the left and he checked his run before cutting inside and finding Quinn who ran on to fire home his second goal of the campaign.

Bury went close to equalising on a couple of occasions and Rovers were indebted to goalkeeper Scott Howie when he kept out a last minute effort from Jon Newby.

Goalscorer Quinn (pictured) never really known as being prolific, claimed afterwards that he had rediscovered his goalscoring touch and set himself a target of equalling his best ever seasonal tally.

'Graham Hyde is playing more of a holding role now so I'm delighted to be able to push forward and if I can get a few more goals it will help us. Three more will do me and equal my best in a season.'

Graydon was delighted to have seen his side win at long last; *'We've lost only two games in 12 now and I'm delighted to come here and win 1-0 against a team going for promotion and do it in classic style.*

'We've looked tighter recently and although we didn't create a lot of chances in front of goal, one is enough if you keep a clean sheet. There's no doubt we have become more difficult to beat.

'I've said it before, but Rob Quinn is our most consistent performer. He gets smacked all over the place but gives everything for the cause.'

Rovers: Howie, Boxall, Barrett, Austin, Anderson, Carlisle, Quinn, Hyde, Street, Di Piedi (Tait), Grazioli (Gilroy).

Substitutes: Parker, Clarke, Astafjevs

An East End Win

Rovers travelled to play Leyton Orient on March 15th 2003 still deep in relegation trouble.

With 11 games remaining they were one of the bottom five clubs separated by just a point. Interestingly, one of those five clubs were Swansea City, soon to embark on a journey all the way to the Premiership (as it was back then), League Cup success and a European sojourn.

Ten points adrift of their opponents, Rovers managed to pull off a surprising win that afternoon, thanks to goals from Giuliano Grazioli and Paul Tait.

In giving one of their best performances of the season Rovers might well have won by a bigger margin. Nevertheless, it was a massive win and there were scenes of jubilation in the Brisbane Road stand housing the 788 Rovers supporters, who celebrated claiming all three points. There were also celebrations on the pitch, as you can see from this photo showing Chairman Geoff Dunford with Vitalijs Astafjevs.

There were 13 minutes on the clock when Grazioli opened the scoring. Sonny Parker's long throw was helped on by Tait and 'Graz' turned and rifled a shot past home keeper Lee Harrison.

There were chances to increase the lead, but they were squandered and Orient equalised from the penalty spot with three minutes of the half remaining.

Chris Tate went down in the box as he prepared to meet a cross from Carl Hutchings and the referee decided that Parker had instigated the fall by tugging his shirt. Former Rovers defender Matt Lockwood stepped up to beat Scott Howie with his spot kick.

A fairly even second period came to life on 70 minutes when Grazioli's volley crashed against the crossbar, but two minutes later Tait scored what proved to be the winning goal.

A corner, taken by substitute Astafjevs, was met by the tall striker and he glanced a header past Harrison and defender Matt Joseph.

As well as Lockwood, Orient fielded former Rovers loanee Ciaran Toner in the lineup, and a future Rovers player in the shape of Lee Thorpe.

Speaking after the game Grazioli, who could well have improved his season's goal tally given the number of chances that came his way, said; 'I should have come away with two match balls, because they weren't half chances that I should have put away.

'But, being a striker, you'd rather miss chances than not get any and I'm glad I had them, glad I scored a goal, and very glad that we got three points.'

His manager was equally pleased, saying; 'I was keeping count of the number of real opportunities we had and got to about 12 before I stopped writing them down.

'As it was, we scored from two set pieces; but I don't care how we do it as long as we win matches.'

Rovers: Howie, Parker, Barrett, Austin, Anderson, Carlisle (Astafjevs), Quinn, Hyde, Llewellyn (Hogg), Tait, Grazioli (Street).

Substitutes: Bryant, Gilroy

Hartlepool Humbled

Following their win against Leyton Orient, Rovers entertained York City in a midweek match at the Memorial Stadium.

However, a 1-0 defeat in that game meant that they were still in trouble at the foot of the league when Hartlepool arrived for a crucial Division Three fixture on March 22nd 2003.

Manager Ray Graydon had freshened up his side by signing Lee Hodges on loan from Rochdale until the end of the season. A product of the West Ham Academy, Hodges had played alongside Rio Ferdinand and Frank Lampard at Upton Park.

He went straight into the side to face Hartlepool and lasted 69 minutes before being replaced by Michele Di Piedi (pictured).

A rare Graham Hyde goal, scored after only seven minutes, gave Rovers all three points in a game watched by a crowd of 6,557.

The visitors were pushing for promotion and were 38 points and 21 places better off than their hosts but it was Rovers who looked the better side in the opening 45 minutes.

Hyde's goal was made in Birmingham as the former Blues midfielder hit a shot high into the roof of the net after Paul Tait's flick on from a throw in taken by Sonny Parker, who had played for Birmingham's reserve side before joining Rovers.

Although well on top, Rovers failed to add to their goal tally and then found themselves under pressure in the second period.

However, goalkeeper Scott Howie who had been a virtual spectator before the break, was in outstanding form and the visitors could find no way past him.

In goal for the Monkey Hangers was former Rovers loanee Anthony Williams, while Darrell Clarke who moved the Memorial Stadium as assistant manager in the summer of 2013, played in midfield and was booked for dissent in the 38th minute!

The three points were a help, but the win still left Graydon's side only two points above the relegation places, one of four teams on 40 points.

Speaking after the game goalscorer Hyde, who missed an opportunity to double his tally midway through the second half, said; *'I was so glad they didn't get an equaliser because I would have laid awake all night worrying about that one.*

'It would have been nice had we gone 2-0 up, got a bit of breathing space and been able to relax. But it wasn't to be, and we had to hang on for the last quarter of an hour.

'It was backs to the wall stuff, but we defended superbly and Scott Howie was magnificent.'

Manager Graydon attributed the win to hard work on the training ground; *'We work hard on our set pieces and spend a lot of time on them.*

'We looked dangerous from the set plays and looked like we were going to score from quite a few of our corners and long throws.'

Rovers: Howie, Parker, Austin, Barrett, Anderson, Astafjevs, Quinn, Hyde, Hodges (Di Piedi), Llewellyn, Tait (Street).

Substitutes: Boxall, Grazioli, Carlisle

Rambo Arrives

With eight games of the season remaining, and his side in deep trouble at the foot of the Third Division table, Ray Graydon made what was probably his most important signing for the club.

Andy Rammell (pictured) a 36 year old striker with dodgy knees, joined Rovers on transfer deadline day in March 2003 and proved to be Rovers' saviour, as he scored four very important goals before the campaign ended, which helped prevent the club sliding into The Conference.

Rammell began his career with non-league outfit Atherstone United before securing a dream move to Manchester United. The £40,000 fee was used by Atherstone to construct a new stand, which they named after their former striker.

After only a year at Old Trafford he moved to Barnsley, who appear to have paid £100,000 to secure his services, though they were repaid with 44 goals in the 185 league games he appeared in whilst at Oakwell.

Next stop was Roots Hall, Southend, and then came a move to Walsall where he became Graydon's first signing after he took over as boss at the Bescot Stadium.

Next port of call was Adams Park, Wycombe, and his debut was one he wasn't to forget in a hurry as he was sent off following a challenge on Rovers' keeper Nick Culkin.

'I apologised to the keeper afterwards, so it was all ok between us and I had the red card rescinded afterwards so I didn't serve a ban, although that didn't help me on the night.'

It was from Wycombe that he moved to the Memorial Stadium and earned himself almost legendary status for scoring the goals that kept the club in league football.

He acknowledged that had it not been for the fact that Graydon was manager he might not have moved to Bristol. Other clubs were interested in signing him, with promotion chasing Kidderminster Harriers only just missing out on securing his signature.

'The chance to work with Ray again was an important part of my decision. He tries to make his sides hard to beat, and I think results over the last few weeks have shown that's what has started to happen.

'That's great from a striker's point of view because it means one goal can often be enough to win you the match and it takes some of the pressure off.

'I'm here to lead the line, get in amongst it, upset defences, bring others into play and, hopefully, chip in with the odd goal.

'If, at the end of eight games I haven't scored but the other striker has got 12 goals, I'll still feel I have done my job.

'If we win every game from now until the end of the season 1-0 and I don't score, I'm sure Ray won't be complaining because results are everything at the moment.

'I'll just do what I'm told; I've learned that much from playing under him before!'

Double Delight

In terms of results, Andy Rammell's first four games for the club weren't at all successful and had yielded a solitary point, from a 1-1 draw against Rochdale at Spotland.

The other three games had ended in defeat, against Lincoln City, Rushden & Diamonds, and Wrexham.

When they entertained Cambridge United, on April 19th 2003, only goal difference was keeping them out of the relegation places and the pressure was on Ray Graydon's side to take all three points.

Two days later, on Easter Monday, they would be travelling to the country's other main university town, Oxford, so it was a make or break weekend.

Cambridge, managed by former Rovers striker John Taylor, were brushed aside in front of a Memorial Stadium crowd of 7,563, Rammell scoring twice in a 3-1 win.

The opening goal came after 29 minutes when the striker raced on to a long clearance from goalkeeper Scott Howie, forced his way past defender Ezomo Iriekpen and touched the ball past Shaun Marshall in the Cambridge goal.

They held that slender lead going into half time but had to wait until the 64th minute before doubling their lead thanks, again, to Rammell. The striker brought down a cross from Chris Llewellyn before beating Marshall from close range.

Nine minutes from time Rovers wrapped up the points when Vitalijs Astafjevs took a pass from Graham Hyde before drilling a low shot past Marshall for goal number three. The visitors did manage to pull a goal back in the last minute, Paul Kitson scoring from the penalty spot after the referee spotted a handball by Hyde in a goalmouth scramble.

Speaking after the game, Graydon said that he had once scored a goal very similar to Rammell's first of the afternoon; 'I got one like that from an Andy Lochead flick on in about 1942!

'You work on passing out on the training ground and then it just shows what happens if a player is prepared to get on the end of one kick from the goalkeeper. I have to say Andy showed a bit of pace I didn't think he still had!'

Rammell (pictured) was still buzzing when he was interviewed; 'When the second goal went in, it typified why I came here because the noise and the fans were just amazing.

'Moments like that give you goosepimples and that's why I play football; that's what keeps you going. You could see how much it means to people and, hopefully, they can see how much it means to me.'

Cambridge boss Taylor was magnanimous in defeat; 'Fair play to Rovers because they worked very hard and made it difficult for us. It's a huge result for them.

'Andy Rammell is a good pro who has been around and showed what he is still capable of out there today. He caused us problems all game and we couldn't handle him.'

Rovers: Howie, Parker, Barrett, Austin (Boxall), Anderson, Astafjevs, Quinn, Hyde, Hodges (Street), Llewellyn, Rammell (Tait).

Substitutes: Grazioli, Carlisle

Just Like The Alamo

Two days after beating Cambridge United Rovers travelled to the Kassam Stadium and made it a Happy Easter, not to mention a University double, by beating Oxford 1-0.

Ray Graydon was returning to a club he had played for and where he spent a number of years as a coach.

Future Rovers players Dave Savage, James Hunt and Jefferson Louis all appeared for Oxford that afternoon while Ian Atkins, who would eventually take over the managerial reins at the Memorial Stadium, was in charge of the U's.

The only goal of the game was scored by Andy Rammell, taking his tally for the weekend to three.

More importantly, the three points lifted Rovers up the table to 20th place, five points clear of relegation.

It was a nail biting 53 minutes for the 3,000 Rovers fans inside the ground before the goal arrived, and an even more anxious 37 minutes waiting for the final whistle.

Rammell struck after Adam Barrett had nodded Sonny Parker's free kick back across goal, firing high into the roof of the net from seven yards.

Graydon's side were under constant pressure for almost the entire 90 minutes and had to dig deep to prevent the home side scoring.

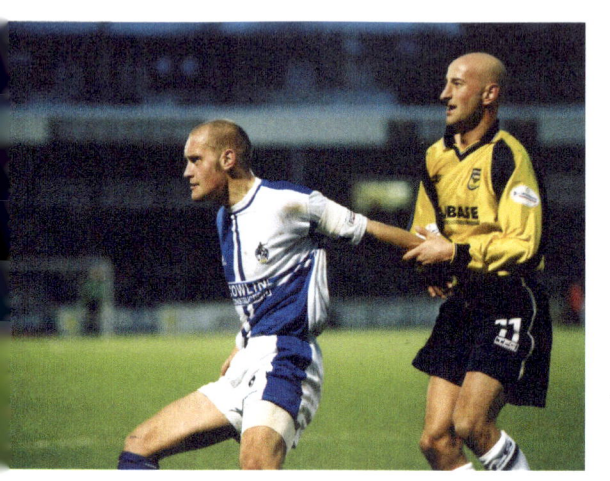

'The Gas are staying up' rang out around the Kassam Stadium at the final whistle, as relegation looked to have been avoided. However, Graydon struck a note of caution in his post-match interview.

'While it's been a great Easter for everyone, we are not safe yet, but I think the fans will feel as confident as I do that things are looking better than they were last week.

'We were probably favourites for one of the two relegation spots before that, now we are one of the favourites to get out of it.

'I'm delighted to be in that situation because these have been two very big results for us.'

The manager acknowledged that his side had defended exceptionally well during the game.

'Oxford made things very difficult and maybe three or four months ago we would have turned around three or four goals down at half time.

'Oxford had chances, but we defended very well in our box and I'm including everyone in that. There were some great blocks, our keeper made some good saves, and we had to continue doing that in the second half.'

There was praise for Adam Barrett (pictured), for Rammell, and for the travelling Gasheads.

'Adam doesn't hold back, he's in your face as a player and he made some fantastic blocks.

'I'm pleased for Andy Rammell, who has come here in the twilight of his career and has taken on the responsibility that I wanted him to.

'Our fans were outsinging Oxford, who are looking at the play offs and at Third Division level that's fantastic. You can't ask for anything more.'

Rovers: Howie, Parker, Barrett, Austin, Anderson, Astafjevs (Street), Quinn, Hyde, Hodges (Carlisle), Llewellyn, Rammell (Tait).

Substitutes: Grazioli, Boxall

Staying Up!

Rovers went into their final home game of the 2002/03 campaign knowing that a third successive win would guarantee Third Division survival.

Ray Graydon's first season in charge had proved to be a traumatic one as it had been hoped that the manager would see his side challenging at the top end of the table, not struggling to avoid relegation into non-league football.

It seems that if you can't be involved in the promotion shake up, then the next best thing to boost home crowds is to be involved in a relegation battle. Perhaps that explains why a crowd of 9,835 turned up at the Mem on April 26th 2003 to see if Graydon could lead his side to safety with victory against Darlington.

The support received that afternoon obviously lifted everyone and Rovers twice managed to beat their former goalkeeper Andy Collett and picked up all three points thanks to a 2-1 victory.

Andy Rammell's fourth goal in three games gave Rovers the lead on 22 minutes. The veteran striker chested down a cross from Wayne Carlisle and drove the ball home from 12 yards and is pictured here in action against Collett in the match.

It was the only goal of the opening 45 minutes, but with relegation rivals Exeter and Carlisle both winning as well, it was vital that Graydon's side held on to their lead.

Although they were playing well, the visitors always looked capable of getting back on level terms and they did just that with 66 minutes on the clock.

Ryan Valentine's cross from the right was punched clear by Scott Howie, but only as far as Clark Keltie, who hit a stunning 25yard shot that flew into the net. A few anxious moments ensued before Carlisle scored the most important goal of his Rovers career.

There were 15 minutes remaining when he 'bent it like Beckham' and curled a free kick around Darlington's defensive wall and past Collett, giving the keeper no chance of saving.

There were a few anxious moments for Rovers and their supporters after that, but Rovers held out for the win, and there were emotional scenes of celebration at the final whistle.

Matchwinner Carlisle, who had to persuade Lee Hodges not to take the all-important free kick, said afterwards; *'It's the most important goal I've ever scored in my life.*

'Hodgey might have thought he was going to take it ...but I knew he wasn't! He put the ball down and placed it, but I'd said before the game that if a free kick came up in that sort of position, I wanted it.'

'I wouldn't say it was a great game to watch, because it was quite scrappy, but we held in there and although Darlington got on top for a spell in the second half, we got the points...so who cares?'

Rovers: Howie, Parker (Boxall), Barrett, Austin, Anderson, Carlisle, Quinn, Hyde (Bryant), Hodges (Street), Llewellyn, Rammell.

Substitutes: Tait, Grazioli

A Draw at Kiddy

With Rovers having secured their Third Division safety the previous week, and Kidderminster's play-off hopes ending the same weekend, the two teams met on the final day of the 2002/03 season with nothing but pride to play for.

There probably wasn't even too much of that around the Aggborough Stadium as several players were aware that they would be leaving the Memorial Stadium in the near future, while others were no doubt dreaming of being on a beach somewhere!

'Kiddy' manager Ian Britton, a Bristolian and a Rovers supporter, was mightily relieved that the Gas didn't have to win to secure their safety, as he admitted he hadn't wanted to be in charge of the side that sent them down to the Conference.

'If it had come to it then I would have sent my team out to win,' he said before this match, *'but I'm just very relieved it hasn't come to that. I know that no one has a divine right to stay in the Football League, but how could a club as big as Rovers go down? It would have been absolutely dreadful, especially for me.'*

The game itself petered out into a 1-1 draw, with JJ Melligan opening the scoring for the home side on 15 minutes and Paul Tait equalising for Rovers 20 minutes from time.

The game was refereed by Howard Webb who booked two players from each side for unsporting behaviour, Kidderminster's Scott Stamps and Danny Williams and Rovers' Chris Llewellyn and Rob Quinn.

Williams was one of three future Rovers players in the Kidderminster lineup, the other two being Craig Hinton and Bo Henriksen.

Manager Ray Graydon said afterwards that he wanted his players to start thinking, and preparing, for the following season.

'We will be training hard for the next few weeks; we won't be going away and switching off now because there is a long pre-season, and I'm trying to make it a bit shorter.

'I want the players to step up their fitness before they go away on holiday, and I want them to come back better prepared than they were last year.

'If we are not in the top two this time next year, I want us to still be working because we are in the play offs.'

Three days later the manager released five members of his squad, Scott Howie, Mark McKeever, Lewis Hogg, Bradley Allen and Trevor Challis, so it's safe to assume that they didn't continue to train hard before their holiday!

Graydon (pictured) also revealed that he was hoping that Sonny Parker, Lee Hodges, Andy Rammell, Chris Llewellyn and Ijah Anderson would stay with the club.

In the meantime, he prepared a side for one final game at the Mem, a testimonial for Roy Dolling in which Rovers beat a Coventry City side 2-1.

Rovers: Howie, Parker, Barrett, Austin, Anderson, Carlisle (Street), Quinn, Bryant, Hodges, Llewellyn, Tait.

Substitutes: Grazioli, Boxall, Gilroy, Hogg

Four Additions

Manager Ray Graydon signed four new players in the summer of 2003, all of whom are pictured here before the season started.

On the left of the photo is defender Christian Edwards who began his career with Swansea City before moving on to Nottingham Forest. He had been out on loan to a number of clubs, including a three game stint at Ashton Gate, before pitching up at the Memorial Stadium.

'Swanny', so called because of his long neck! said; *'Obviously the main reason for coming here is to play regular first team football, but alongside that is the level of support the club gets.*

'Through friends of mine, I know that the fans are passionate about their club and that, allied to the fact that I think we have a good team here, were other reasons for wanting to come here.'

He went on to appear in 99 league games and since leaving he has gained a First Class Degree in sports coaching, completed a Masters Degree and a PhD and managed the Cardiff Met side in the Welsh Premier League.

Falmouth born goalkeeper Kevin Miller played only 30 minutes of pre-season football after undergoing keyhole surgery on a torn cartilage. He went on to make 72 league appearances for the club before his departure.

His career began at Exeter and he moved on to play for Birmingham City, Watford, Crystal Palace and Barnsley before returning to St James' Park. He extended his league career with spells at Derby County, Southampton and Torquay United41 before going on to make over 200 appearances for Bodmin Town.

On joining Rovers, he said; *'I feel very positive about the season ahead and I wouldn't have come here if I felt it was going to be another struggle.'*

Sitting next to Miller is former Millwall, Northampton Town and Oxford United midfielder Dave Savage was also looking forward to the season ahead; *'Pre-season has been good and we had a week away together where everyone bonded really well. We are all looking forward to the start of competitive football. I feel a buzz about the place, and I can't wait for everything to get underway.'*

The Republic of Ireland international was to spend two years at the Memorial Stadium, appearing in 65 league games, before moving on to Rushden & Diamonds. He then wound down his playing career on the non-league scene, first with Brackley Town and then, finally, with Oxford City.

Junior Agogo is the man on the right of the photo. The striker certainly had a knack of scoring goals and the ability to have played at the top level, but he never quite made it. Three years at Rovers yielded 41 goals in 126 league games before a move to Nottingham Forest where he won the first of his 27 caps for Ghana.

On the eve of his first season at the Mem, he said; *'I'm looking forward to scoring in games that matter and really looking forward to the season ahead.'*

Sadly, Junior passed away in August 2019 at the age of 40.

The Stretcher Race

Manager Ray Graydon was known in some quarters as the 'sergeant major' so it came as little surprise that he took his players to the Azimghur Army Barracks at Colerne for pre-season training in the summer of 2003.

The manager had used the base the previous summer, and it was to become Rovers' training ground. Situated some 20 miles outside of Bristol, it was hardly the ideal venue, though it had everything needed for a football club to train in complete privacy as the armed guards on the gate saw to it that no one without the required pass got through!

This particular article, though, looks at the training Graydon's team endured that summer and it must have been a wakeup call for some of his new recruits, who included Junior Agogo, Dave Savage, Christian Edwards.

Agogo arrived from Barnet for a fee in the region of £110,000 funded entirely from the Share Scheme. The venture, launched the previous December, had already been used to part fund the wages of another striker, Andy Rammell at the end of the previous campaign.

Steve Burns, at that time an Associate Director, said; 'The beauty of the Agogo deal is that it is payable over two years and at the moment around £600 per week is going towards it.

'To be able to buy a player for that sort of money shows just how quickly the scheme has snowballed and it is excellent news.'

Two of the new boys, Edwards and Savage, are pictured here in the group taking part in the stretcher race during the week long stay at Colerne.

Essentially, it was a two mile race carrying a stretcher loaded with water cans weighing 16 stone and this was the winning team, with Sonny Parker, Danny Greaves, Danny Boxall, Dave Gilroy, Kevin Street, and Shane Hobbs accompanying the new lads.

The thoughts of Savage are not recorded, but those of Edwards were interesting, to say the least!

'Nobody told me about the army camp thing until after I had signed, so to say it was a bit of a surprise when I was told where we'd be starting pre-season training was an understatement!

'I have never been to one before and it has certainly opened my eyes a bit. There have been some tough tasks, such as diving into the swimming pool fully clothed to be shown how to survive in a disaster.

'Nothing, though, has been harder than the stretcher race, and I'm sure the other lads feel the same way.'

Graydon was pleased with the work undertaken by his squad; 'We are enjoying some lovely facilities here, for getting together, talking about our football, and doing some ball work too in the wide open spaces.

'I am delighted with our new recruits and everyone is in good heart. Maybe that has something to do with the fact we haven't lost a game yet!'

Opening Day Win

In spite of a mixed bag of pre-season results, Rovers got off to a winning start in their first game of the 2003/04 campaign, beating Scunthorpe United 2-1 at Glanford Park where former Scunthorpe player Lee Hodges scored the winning goal.

Although they bowed out of the Carling Cup at the first round stage, to Brighton, Graydon's side remained undefeated in the league until the end of August when they suffered a home defeat against Huddersfield Town.

The opening fixture against Scunthorpe took place on August 9th and Graydon was already missing Andy Rammell through injury, whilst awaiting the outcome of fitness tests on Junior Agogo, Graham Hyde and Wayne Carlisle.

Hyde was the only one of that trio who failed to make the trip, but Agogo and Carlisle took their places in a starting lineup that saw four players, Kevin Miller, Christian Edwards, Dave Savage and Agogo make their debuts while a fifth new boy, loanee Callum Willock, was on the bench.

The first goal of the new campaign was scored by skipper Adam Barrett after 12 minutes. Wayne Carlisle's free kick was blocked by Scunthorpe's defensive wall, but the loose ball fell to Kevin Street, who chipped the ball to Edwards and he nodded back across goal where Barrett headed past home goalkeeper Tom Evans.

Graydon's side held their lead until the 63rd minute, when Peter Beagrie equalised from the penalty spot after Ijah Anderson was adjudged to have fouled Matt Sparrow.

With 13 minutes remaining Rovers introduced Hodges (pictured) in place of Street and the former Scunthorpe favourite was loudly booed by the fans who used to cheer him week in, week out.

However, he had the last laugh as four minutes from time he pounced on Danny Boxall's deflected cross and gleefully rolled the ball into the net from close range.

The celebrations were wild and afterwards he explained why he had ripped off his shirt to mark his first 'Gas' goal.

'I wish I hadn't done it now, but that goal meant so much to me. There was so much emotion involved I just went mad. I could have stripped naked because my head just went. It wasn't that I'd come off the bench to score against my old club, but the fact that it happened so late in the game and got us the three points we wanted.

'I thought I'd let the rest of the lads do all the hard work and then come on for the last 15 minutes and nick all the glory!'

It was the first time in eight years that Rovers had won an away game on the first day of a new season and manager Graydon was delighted with the victory.

'It's a feather in our cap going there and taking three points because there won't be too many teams who do it. They are a very good side.'

Rovers: Miller, Boxall, Barrett, Edwards, Anderson, Carlisle, Quinn, Savage, Street (Hodges), Tait, Agogo (Willock).

Substitutes: Austin, Parker, Clarke

Carlisle 0 Carlisle 2

It was the story that made all the headlines the following day as Wayne Carlisle scored both goals to beat the club bearing his surname and is seen here celebrating with Rob Quinn!

The game was played on August 23rd 2003 at Brunton Park and the three points meant that Rovers ended the day in fourth place, unbeaten in their first three league games.

Carlisle's Chairman at the time was Irish billionaire John Courtenay who had installed Roddy Collins, brother of a former world boxing champion, as manager.

Manager Ray Graydon was able to name an unchanged side for a fourth successive game and he sent his side out wearing their new black and yellow away strip.

Rovers took a 38th minute lead after Paul Tait was bundled to the ground by a home defender as he battled for possession just outside the area.

Carlisle stepped up to strike a stunning free kick which took former Rovers loan goalkeeper Matt Glennon by surprise and the shot stopper could only watch as the ball flew past him.

Two minutes before half time Carlisle struck again with his, and Rovers', second goal of the afternoon.

Dave Savage threaded the ball through to Junior Agogo, whose cross found Carlisle and he had the simple task of netting from close range.

Rovers defended their lead comfortably after the break, much to the frustration of all but the 325 Gasheads in the crowd of 4,674.

Graydon, who had come under fire in the build-up to the game because of his apparent inflexibility when it came to allowing his players to be interviewed, and the fact that training took place at an Army Barracks, sent assistant boss John Still to the post-match press conference.

'It was a good away performance,' said the amiable number two, adding 'now we have to start winning our home games as well.

'We've worked very hard on our teamwork, organisation and discipline over the past year and now I think it's beginning to show'.

Of Carlisle's first goal, Still said; 'It was a great strike but probably no great surprise to us because we've seen him do it before and know what he's capable of. In a way, the second was even more enjoyable because it was a good team goal.'

Meanwhile, the goalscorer had this to say; 'I didn't actually see the first one go in, but I could tell from where the keeper was standing that he'd left me too much room. I just hit it and then the next thing I heard was the cheer from our fans.

'As for the second one, it came from good football and in the first half, in particular, we managed to break them down and get through a few times and I was lucky enough to be there to tuck it away.'

Rovers: Miller, Boxall, Barrett, Edwards, Anderson, Carlisle (Hyde), Quinn, Savage, Street, Tait, Agogo (Willock).

Substitutes: Bryant, Parker, Austin

A Boston Bashing

A 1-0 Bank Holiday Monday win over Kidderminster Harriers saw Rovers move up to fifth place in the table and that was followed by another home game, against Boston United, on September 13th 2003

Prior to that game there was a great deal of speculation regarding a possible groundshare with Bristol City in a new, purpose built, stadium. An organisation called Gloucestershire Arenas had been formed to develop plans for a 30,000 all seater arena to be built alongside a smaller, 10,000 capacity seat oval venue on the same site.

Everything was to be built on a parcel of land to the east of the M49, near Easter Compton and although it sounded an exciting project, it never did get off the ground.

As talk of the new stadium rumbled on into a second week, it was reported that fans of both Rovers and City were in favour of the development and had given it a 'cautious' welcome.

As always, though, there were objections of the political variety and Northavon Liberal Democrat MP Steve Webb was one who was opposed to the project.

And, so, we move swiftly on to the game against Boston and a 2-0 win moved the club up to the giddy heights of third place, but that was to be as good as it got all season!

Lewis Haldane had scored a hat trick and Wayne Carlisle twice in a 5-1 win in a midweek reserve game against Oxford United, though neither were in the starting lineup to face Boston, although Carlisle was on the bench.

Shrewsbury Town striker Nigel Jemson also featured in that reserve game, as it was thought that Ray Graydon was interested in signing him, though the manager's interest appeared to wane after the match.

A goalless first half did against Boston did nothing to please the crowd of 6,845, who had to wait until the 67th minute for the first goal of the afternoon.

Wayne Carlisle delivered a free kick into the area and although Adam Barrett stooped to get in a header, Paul Tait got the final touch and steered the ball past goalkeeper Paul Bastock.

The game was all but won ten minutes from time when Tait's header appeared to take a deflection off of defender Mark Greaves on its way past Bastock.

Junior Agogo is pictured in action during the match.

Assistant manager John Still was the man to speak to the press afterwards and he said; *'I think we eventually ground Boston down and got on top.*

'When we did that, we started to play some better football. However, Boston paid us a lot of respect because we had them watched twice and both times they had played a 4-4-2 system.

'Here they came with three centre halves and defenders very deep to stop us getting in behind them. They made it very difficult for us to break them down, but we will probably get that from a lot of teams this season.'

Rovers: Miller, Boxall, Barrett, Edwards, Anderson, Savage, Quinn (Carlisle), Hyde, Hodges (Street), Tait, Agogo.

Substitutes: Austin, Bryant, Parker

Haldane's Debut

Successive away defeats at opposite ends of the country, Torquay and York, had left Rovers in ninth place, but they returned to winning ways when they entertained Cheltenham Town on September 27th 2003.

A 2-0 win against the Gloucestershire Robins, in front of a Memorial Stadium crowd of 8,303, was achieved with goals from Paul Tait and Wayne Carlisle.

There was a distinct Bristol feel about the side put out by Cheltenham, as they named six former City players in their squad and two former Rovers players, namely goalkeeper Shane Higgs and Lee Howells while Steve Book, a future Rovers goalkeeping coach, was on the bench.

Tait was on target with two minutes of the first half remaining, powering home a header from Danny Boxall's pinpoint cross. It was the striker's fifth goal of the season.

Lewis Haldane, pictured on his Rovers debut after going on as an 85th minute substitute, was involved in Rovers' second goal, scored from the penalty spot by Carlisle three minutes from time.

The young Rovers striker chased down a long ball from Kevin Miller and was upended by Higgs, and Carlisle sent the keeper the wrong way with his spot kick.

Carlisle injured an ankle in the game, and manager Ray Graydon was afraid that might mean changing his lineup for the game against Mansfield three days later; *'Wayne picked up a nasty whack on his lower limb and his ankle has swollen up horribly.'*

The manager was pleased, though, that Haldane had made his debut; *'It was great to see a young kid come on and give us a threat and win us a penalty.*

'What he did is what he's good at; that's his game, although the rest of it needs improvement.

'He doesn't give a ball up and he's got the pace to worry defenders when the ball goes in behind them.

'He's probably the only one in the club who would have won us that penalty.'

There were also words of encouragement for Haldane from Carlisle, who also told how he had to beat Tait to the ball when the penalty was awarded.

'Lewis did really well. He's been scoring for the reserves. He's awkward and he's quick, and with his sort of pace he can cause defenders problems at this level.

Now he's just got to get his head down and work.'

Of the penalty he said; *'You have got to fancy yourself from the spot. I think Paul Tait wanted this one, but I got to the ball first!*

'He and Giuliano Grazioli missed a couple last season, so I've taken them since and I'm happy to carry on…I won't say until I miss one, because that's not going to happen!'

Rovers: Miller, Boxall, Barrett, Edwards, Anderson, Carlisle, Savage, Hyde (Quinn), Hodges (Street), Tait, Agogo (Haldane).

Substitutes: Parker, Austin

Darlo Defeated

Having suffered a 5-1 mauling at the hands of Doncaster Rovers the previous week, Rovers travelled to the north east to face Darlington on October 11th 2003 and claimed all three points with an emphatic 4-0 win.

The Reynolds Arena hosted a crowd of 4,268 that afternoon, but they were still lost in the 20,000+ all seater stadium built, and named, after their dubious benefactor George Reynolds.

Handed his first start for the club, Lewis Haldane scored his second senior goal, putting Rovers ahead after 37 minutes.

Following a free kick into the Darlington area, Paul Tait managed to find Haldane and he lashed a shot into the net beyond the reach of goalkeeper Michael Price.

Tait was again the provider for the second Rovers goal, which arrived on 64 minutes. This time the striker headed Wayne Carlisle's corner back across goal to Dave Savage (pictured) who beat Price from 15 yards.

Tait made way for Andy Rammell, making his first appearance of the season, on 74 minutes and he scored with his first touch when he rose unchallenged to meet Carlisle's corner three minutes later and headed home from close range.

With a minute of the game remaining Rammell scored again when he headed Carlisle's cross past Price from six yards.

The win pushed Ray Graydon's side up to ninth place, but it was to be November 29th before they claimed their next victory and by that time they had been knocked out of the LDV Vans Trophy by Southend United and suffered defeat at Bournemouth in the first round of the FA Cup.

The manager was under pressure as another unsuccessful campaign beckoned, and he was well aware that it would take more than the win at Darlington to appease his critics.

'There will always be critics when you are losing, that's the nature of the game we are in.

'The only way you can change that is by being successful and that's what I'm trying to achieve with this club.'

He also appeared to wonder whether or not time was on his side.

'If directors appoint a manager and have confidence in him, then they should stick with him because it's a long term job.

'If you spoke to any manager he would tell you that three years is long enough to get close to where you want to be. But it's not often you get three years.'

The goals that Rammell scored that day were to be his last for the club, though he wasn't to know that at the time; *'I only knew I was going to be on the bench on the morning of the game. It felt great to get on and score two goals, but my performance was only the icing on the cake. The other lads did all the hard work and set things up for me.'*

Rovers: Miller, Boxall, Barrett, Edwards, Anderson, Carlisle, Savage, Hyde (Austin), Quinn, Tait (Rammell), Haldane (Street).

Substitutes: Parker, Uddin

A Win At Last

Rovers entertained Hull City on November 29th 2003, seeking their first win in over a month.

A crowd of 6,331 were inside the Memorial Stadium to see Ray Graydon's side clinch victory with a 2-1 win.

It was to be the side's last home win of 2003 and Graydon had only a few more months at the helm.

One Rovers player who was relishing the opportunity of facing Hull was Ryan Williams (pictured in action against Hull's Jason Price), who had joined the club on loan from the Tigers in October.

The visitors to north Bristol that afternoon were favourites for promotion but Rovers managed to upset the odds and won, with Williams managing to get on the scoresheet against his parent club, and Junior Agogo netting the other in a 2-1 win.

Graydon's side had to do it the hard way, though, as the visitors opened the scoring with only five minutes on the clock, thanks to a close range header from Ben Burgess following a cross by Ryan France.

Williams struck on 33 minutes after he cut in from the left and fired in a diagonal shot which beat goalkeeper Paul Musselwhite who seemed to be distracted by Agogo's attempt to get his head on the ball.

Both Rovers players seemed to claim the goal, though it was eventually awarded to the diminutive Williams.

'I was just trying to put the ball into the danger area. Junior got across and put the keeper off, but he was quite a way from the ball. Ask the other lads and they will tell you he was nowhere near it. I knew straight away it was my goal.'

Hull boss Peter Taylor must have rued his decision to permit Williams to play in the game, because it was his corner that led to Agogo scoring what proved to be the winning goal.

The visitors didn't clear the ball and it ran to Agogo who smashed it home from close range.

Not surprisingly, his beleaguered manager seemed pretty relieved with the win; 'This was a big game for us and if we can reproduce the best parts of what we have done in our last three games, we'll have an opportunity to win matches.

'At 1-1 we were treading on eggshells again after the way things have gone for us recently, but it was a very good win against a very good team.

'Having given away an early goal, the fans could have got on the players' backs or had a go at me, but they stuck with the players who clawed their way back and deservedly went on to win.

'In the second half, I thought we looked very sharp breaking from defence and looked capable of scoring every time we went forward.'

Rovers: Miller, Parker, Barrett, Edwards, Anderson, Carlisle, Savage, Hyde, Williams, Haldane (Quinn), Agogo.

Substitutes: Boxall, Austin, Tait, Clarke

Boxing Day Blues

Less than two weeks before their Boxing Day 2003 clash with Northampton Town, Rovers axed assistant manager John Still as the club attempted to bring their finances under control.

Still, speaking about his departure, said; *'I have thoroughly enjoyed the 18 months I spent with the club, but to be honest my job was becoming a bit frustrating because the financial situation meant we weren't able to do a lot of the things I thought needed to be done.'*

Manager Ray Graydon was disappointed to be losing his right hand man; *'The decision wasn't anything I had a say in. If I did, then John would have been staying here for a very long time.*

'It was a board decision and a financial one, and very difficult for all of us at the football club to take. I think our loss is going to be someone else's gain.'

Initially, Still's departure had no effect, as Rovers beat Southend 1-0 at Roots Hall on December 20th. However, they returned to losing ways on Boxing Day in front of a Memorial Stadium crowd of 7,695.

Although they lost the game 2-1, Rovers had a number of chances to pick up all three points but two lapses of concentration at the back cost them dearly.

There was never any hint of what was to come as, after a goalless first half, Wayne Carlisle put them in front from the penalty spot just a minute after the restart.

When Lewis Haldane went down in the box, Graydon's players appealed, somewhat half-heartedly, for a penalty that was surprisingly given by referee Phil Prosser and Carlisle thumped his spot kick past goalkeeper Lee Harper.

The visitors equalised 15 minutes from time, when Chris Willmott's ball over the top found Derek Asamoah in space and he hit a shot into the top corner of the net from 20 yards.

Four minutes from time the defence failed to deal with Willmott's header into the box and allowed Richard Walker time and space to shoot past Kevin Miller for the winning goal. Four years later the same player would be a Rovers hero in a Wembley play off final.

Also in the Northampton side that day was man who would manage the side at Wembley, Paul Trollope, while another member of Rovers' Wembley squad, Chris Carruthers, appeared as a second half substitute for the Cobblers.

Rovers skipper Adam Barrett is pictured, closely watched by Richard Walker.

'Defeat,' said Graydon afterwards, *'was very difficult to take because everyone will have gone away wondering how we've not won three of our last four games.*

'Some aspects of our play were very good indeed because we got quality balls into the area. But I can't do anything else to get people to score apart from standing beside them in the penalty area.

'If we are going to win games then we have to take our chances.'

Rovers: Miller, Parker, Barrett, Edwards, Anderson, Carlisle, Savage, Hyde, Williams, Haldane, Agogo (Gilroy).

Substitutes: Austin, Quinn, Hobbs, Clarke

A Loan, A Defeat, And Goodbye!

The week leading up to the game at Macclesfield Town on Tuesday January 14th 2004 was newsworthy for two reasons, and they both concerned strikers!

At the beginning of the week it was announced that Andy Rammell had been told that his playing days were over. The 36 year old striker was to enter hospital for the 13th knee operation of his career. It would keep him out for the remainder of the season and the medical advice was that he should retire.

Only hours before kick off at Moss Rose, manager Ray Graydon signed a new striker, Lee Matthews (pictured), on loan from arch rivals Bristol City. It was a surprise to everyone, not least the rest of Graydon's squad, as the first they knew of his arrival was when he boarded the team coach heading for Cheshire.

He made his debut a few hours later and ended up on the losing side as the Silkmen ran out 2-1 winners. A paltry crowd of 1,542, including 140 Rovers fans, were there to see the game and witnessed a decent performance from 11th placed Rovers.

The new striker almost gave his side the lead eight minutes before half time when he met Wayne Carlisle's cross and glanced a header towards the bottom corner of the goal. However, he was denied by home goalkeeper Steve Wilson who somehow managed to touch the ball away as far as Junior Agogo. With the goal at his mercy, though, the striker screwed his shot wide of the target.

Four minutes later Macclesfield took the lead when Matthew Tipton mishit his shot, totally wrong footing goalkeeper Kevin Miller, who watched helplessly as the ball trickled into the net.

Rovers equalised just after the hour mark when Matthews turned inside his marker and sent a ferocious 25 yard drive towards goal. Wilson managed to touch his effort on to the crossbar, but Lewis Haldane was on hand to pick up the rebound and score from close range.

The game was over on 73 minutes, though, when Rovers defenders backed off, allowing John Miles time and space to curl a shot past Miller.

Graydon was delighted with his new signing;
'The new boy got better as the game went on.
'He was good in the air, held the ball up well and brought other players into the game.'

It was his final Bristol Rovers press conference.

Phil Bater took charge of the side that drew 2-2 at Rochdale four days later, and on January 19th it was announced that Graydon and Rovers had parted company by mutual consent.

Speaking of the announcement, one senior player said; *'The players had lost confidence in the manager months ago. People knew he had a reputation as a disciplinarian, but there were times when the players were treated like naughty kids.'*

Rovers: Miller, Parker, Austin, Barrett, Anderson, Carlisle, Savage (Bryant), Hyde, Williams, Agogo (Haldane), Matthews.

Substitutes: Edwards, Quinn, Tait

Phil's First Win

Following Ray Graydon's departure caretaker boss Phil Bater began his second stint in charge with a draw at Rochdale and a home win against Carlisle United.

He was aware that his stay in the post might not last any longer and speaking before the Carlisle game Phil, pictured here with his assistant, Tony Ricketts, said; 'The situation with me at the moment is completely results orientated,

'If we win on Saturday, I might get the job for another week. If we lose it could be Goodnight Irene.

'I can't compete with many of the names that have been mentioned in regard to the vacancy, but I know Bristol Rovers and I'm not a career man.

'If another job comes up somewhere else in the country I won't be going for it, because I want to manage Bristol Rovers. Now I feel I'm ready for it, whereas I wasn't before.'

Ricketts, a former Bath City player and manager who also turned out for Yeovil Town and coached youth and women's sides, had recently been appointed as Director of Football at Filton College.

The game against Carlisle was played at the Memorial Stadium on January 24th 2004, in front of a crowd of 8,485 and for the second time that season the visitors were shot down by a player bearing the same name as the town.

Wayne Carlisle scored the only goal of the match, netting a 50th minute penalty awarded after Lewis Haldane was fouled by Kevin Gray.

Victory left the side in 12th position in Division Three and there was a feeling of optimism around the place that Bater could take the club further up the table.

Speaking after the win against the Cumbrians, midfielder Dave Savage praised the fans and the new managerial regime; *'The fans were brilliant and were right behind us from the start, probably because there's a new man at the helm.*

'Training was really good last week and we worked on some of the things the players didn't feel were right about their game.

'Tony Ricketts had his say too and the players had an input, but the final decision is going to be down to Phil and that's the way it should be.'

The caretaker boss was also pleased to have secured victory, saying afterwards; 'It was a very emotional day for me, and I've not heard the fans make a noise like that for a long time.

'They were fantastic, but that's just an inkling of what this club could be about if we could get a bit of success. I thought the crowd would get behind the players, but I wasn't expecting to get that sort of reception myself.

'I had a tear or two in my eye and a couple of the lads were taking the mickey out of me because of it.'

Rovers: Miller, Boxall, Barrett, Edwards, Austin, Carlisle, Savage, Hyde, Williams (Agogo), Haldane (Quinn), Matthews (Tait).

Substitutes: Bryant, Clarke

All Change At The Mem

Following the win against Carlisle United on January 24th, Rovers didn't win again until March 27th and by then they were searching for another manager.

Phil Bater's last game in charge was at Boston United on March 20th, when his side lost 1-0.

Press reports indicate that Bater was told he wouldn't be getting the manager's job on a permanent basis prior to the Boston game, and there were strong rumours that Ian Atkins, then in charge at Oxford United, would be the next manager of the club.

The club did confirm that Atkins would be in charge for the start of the 2004/05 campaign but plans to unveil him as the new boss were scuppered when he was suspended by the U's.

Bater's final game at the helm isn't one that he will particularly want to recall as, in an awful game at Boston's York Street, his side went down without a fight to a single goal defeat.

The loss left the club just three points above the relegation zone and once again there were very real fears that the Memorial Stadium might be hosting Conference football the following season.

At a press conference convened just two days after the Boston debacle, Russell Osman and Kevan Broadhurst (pictured either side of Director Steve Burns) were confirmed as joint caretaker managers. Osman was a former Bristol City player and manager while Broadhurst had previously been in charge of Northampton Town.

Bater and his assistant for the 12 games he had been in charge, Tony Ricketts, were to return to their previous jobs, Bater as Rovers youth team coach, Ricketts as Director of Football at Filton College.

With transfer deadline day just four days away Osman confirmed that the club would seek to bring in new faces before then; *'We want to bring in new faces by Thursday so it's going to be a busy time on the training field and in the office. If we do bring people in, we have to integrate them into the team very quickly.'*

Broadhurst said; *'I am here for eight games and that's it, what happens then is up to the board.'* In spite of his denials, he was strongly tipped to be assistant to Atkins once everything had been sorted.

In the meantime, though, he and Osman set about recruiting new players ahead of the deadline and the home game against York City two days after that.

The first to arrive were Ali Gibb and Aaron Lescott, both from Stockport County. Gibb's contract with County had been cancelled, while Lescott signed on loan until the end of the season.

John Anderson also arrived, from Hull City, on a short term deal that took him up until the end of the season.

There were two more as well, though Kidderminster's Danny Williams and Bo Henriksen only arrived at the Mem just five minutes before the 5.00pm deadline, rolling up in Henriksen's dilapidated Ford Escort after getting lost somewhere in Bristol!

New Boys On The Block!

The five new signings made on transfer deadline day 2004 joined two more relative newcomers in Gary Twigg and Lee Thorpe.

Twigg, on loan from Derby County, made eight league appearances before returning to his parent club.

A defender then, he later played for Airdrie United, Oxford United, Hamilton Academical and Brechin City before moving to Ireland where he played for Shamrock Rovers, and later Portadown and Coleraine.

Thorpe, a striker, arrived at Rovers from Leyton Orient, having previously turned out for Blackpool, Bangor, Lincoln City and Grimsby Town.

After four goals in 35 league games at the Mem he continued his nomadic career at Swansea City, Peterborough United, Torquay United, Brentford, Rochdale, Darlington, Fleetwood Town and AFC Fylde, before becoming Youth Development Coach at Blackpool

Defender John Anderson joined Rovers from Hull City having previously played football in his native Scotland, for Greenock Morton and Livingston.

He went on to appear in 54 league games for Rovers and at one point gave up playing to assist Paul Trollope at the helm prior to the arrival of Lennie Lawrence as Director of Football. Since leaving the club he has managed North Ferriby United, been Lead Development Coach at Hull, managed Leeds United U-18's and is now back looking after the Hull U-18 squad.

The 'Stockport Two', Ali Gibb and Aaron Lescott enjoyed rather longer Rovers careers.

Midfielder Gibb began his career as a trainee with Norwich City but had to move to Northampton in order to play league football. From there he joined Stockport County and then spent two years at the Memorial Stadium, making a total of 64 league appearances.

There was a brief spell with Notts County before a move into non-league football, with Bath City. A broken ankle, sustained during pre-season training with the Romans in the summer of 2008, effectively ended his career. He is currently a physiotherapist with Bolton Wanderers.

Lescott spent six years with Rovers and appeared in over 200 games. The former Aston Villa trainee had played for Lincoln City and Sheffield Wednesday before moving to Stockport County and played for Cheltenham Town, Walsall and Halesowen Town after leaving the Memorial Stadium.

The Kidderminster Harriers duo of Danny Williams and Bo Henriksen (pictured with John Anderson) made just nine and four Rovers league appearances respectively.

Former Welsh U-21 midfielder Williams, whose career began at Liverppool, had a two year stint at Wrexham and a loan spell Doncaster Rovers before joining 'Kiddy'. He had been on loan at Chester City before pitching up at the Mem.

On his departure from the Mem he returned to Wrexham and then played for Droylsden, Bala Town and Denbigh Town.

Danish midfielder Henriksen arrived in this country after playing for Odense BK and Herfloge BK and was a popular player whilst with Kidderminster.

He was to appear in just four games for Rovers before returning, first of all, to Denmark and then to Iceland. (He was appointed manager of Danish Superliga side FC Mitjylland in May 2001) He is currently Head Coach at FC Zurich (Switzerland).

A Vital Win

The first game under joint caretaker managers Russell Osman and Kevan Broadhurst took place at the Memorial Stadium on March 27th 2004.

A crowd of 6,723 turned up to see if Rovers could beat York City, one of the teams near them at the foot of the league.

In fact, the Minstermen were two places and one point better off than their hosts before kick-off, though their situation worsened after a 3-0 home win lifted spirits amongst Rovers' supporters.

Four of the five transfer deadline day signings, John Anderson, Ali Gibb (pictured), Aaron Lescott and Danny Williams were in the starting lineup and the fifth, Bo Henriksen, was on the bench.

Rovers took the lead after 19 minutes through Williams, who drove the ball into the net from 20 yards.

Skipper Adam Barrett doubled his side's lead a minute later when he headed home from a Gary Twigg free kick.

If York were on the ropes at half time, they were out for the count a minute into the second half when another debut boy, Gibb, picked up a pass from Lee Thorpe and struck an angled drive past goalkeeper Chris Porter from the edge of the area.

The new boys were full of enthusiasm after the game and Gibb said; *'I had no hesitation in coming here and it would be nice to look back after my career has finished and be able to say I kept Bristol Rovers up.'*

The hero of the hour, though, was Williams. In addition to his goal, he picked up the Supporters Club Man of the Match Award and was mobbed by fans when he entered the Clubhouse Bar to collect his memento of the occasion.

He admitted he had been overwhelmed by the reception he was afforded by a good number of happy Gasheads; *'That was an unbelievable experience. I'm shaking a little bit and I've never known anything like it I didn't know what a Gashead was before the game, but I'm one of them now.*

'The fans were tremendous and to get such a good crowd when we are struggling at the bottom of the league is amazing. I'd played in front of that many for Liverpool reserves, but that doesn't compare to a league game like that, on my debut.

'Once we settled in, we played well and if we can keep that going then we will get out of trouble.'

Osman, the caretaker who was assigned to deal with the media, revealed the players had been treated to an Italian meal the day before the game.

'You can only do so much on a Friday when everyone is getting to know each other for the first time, so we went to an Italian restaurant just to get another half hour together, sat down and had some nice food.'

Rovers: Miller, Edwards, Anderson, Barrett, Austin, Gibb, Williams (D), Lescott, Twigg (Quinn), Agogo (Henriksen), Thorpe (Tait).

Substitutes: Williams (R), Clarke

A Win At Whaddon Road

Following the vital win against York City, Rovers travelled to Whaddon Road on April 3rd 2004 to take on Cheltenham Town and a 2-1 win saw them achieve back to back wins for only the second time that season.

All three goals arrived in the first half and Rovers had to come from behind to claim victory.

The Robins took the lead on the half hour mark when a free kick taken by Grant McCann reached Richard Forsyth. He, in turn, picked out John Brough who slotted the ball past Kevin Miller.

The home side held the lead for only four minutes as skipper Adam Barrett met a cross from Kevin Austin and hit a curling left foot shot past former Rovers goalkeeper Shane Higgs.

The goal that decided the game arrived two minutes before half time. When Gary Twigg's throw in reached Kevin Austin, he delivered a cross into the box that was met by Junior Agogo, who powered a header past Higgs.

Although they hit the crossbar in the second half, Rovers were under a great deal of pressure from the home side and goalkeeper Miller came to their rescue on more than one occasion.

Barrett (pictured), an inspirational captain during his two year stint at the Memorial Stadium, never gave anything less than 100% for the team spoke afterwards about his delight at scoring the opening goal; *'When Kevin put the ball across, I was just trying to send it towards goal.*

'I'll say I meant it to go in the far corner, and the rest of the lads will say I'm a liar!

'We've had a problem with consistency all season, so we really wanted to come here, put in another performance and, most importantly, get three more points.

'The club was getting stuck in a rut and it was hard to see where the next win was coming from. Now we've got new faces in, it's given the place a lift and everybody is fighting for each other.

'It's been two big wins for us in a row and now we've got a couple of tough games over the Easter period. But if we can take another three or four points from them, I'm sure we'll be getting well clear of danger.'

Victory lifted Rovers up to 15th place in the table and one of the two caretaker bosses, Russell Osman, was looking for two Easter wins to secure Division Three safety, saying; *'I thought Cheltenham was a giant step forward for us not only in taking the points, but coming from behind and putting two good results back to back.'*

A 2-1 home defeat against Doncaster Rovers and a goalless draw at Mansfield Town over Easter saw the club drop two places in the league standings, but the battle for survival was almost won.

Rovers: Miller, Austin, Barrett, Edwards, Anderson (J), Gibb, Lescott, Williams, Twigg (Anderson (I)), Thorpe (Haldane), Agogo (Quinn).

Substitutes: Henriksen, Clarke

Swans Sent Packing

The build up to the game against Swansea City on April 17th 2004 saw many within the club state that they felt one more win would be enough to guarantee Third Division safety for another season.

Assistant caretaker boss Kevan Broadhurst said; *'I think another three points now should be enough and we have four games in which to do that.*

'We are still very confident that things are going in the right direction, and if we carry on in the same way that we played in the last two, then we should be OK.

'I see where we are now as a short term problem and the sooner we get it sorted the better.

'I can see only happy days ahead for this football club, and I am sure that next season Rovers will go on to challenge at the right end of the table.'

Central defender Christian Edwards shared that view; *'I think we need another three points to guarantee safety, but the way we are playing at the moment means we could finish well clear of the relegation zone.'*

The three points were duly gained against Swansea, as Rovers again came from behind to claim victory.

The visitors took an eighth minute lead when Paul Connor hit an angled drive past Kevin Miller following good work by Lee Trundle.

Rovers were back on level terms just ten minutes later when Bo Henriksen played in Graham Hyde and he drilled a low shot past Roger Freestone from 25 yards.

The goal that most of the crowd of 7,843 had been waiting for finally arrived on 82 minutes when a neat exchange of passes between substitutes Paul Tait and Junior Agogo ended with Agogo (pictured leaving Roberto Martinez in his wake!) cutting in from the left before hitting a fierce shot past Freestone.

Russell Osman, the other assistant caretaker boss spoke after the final whistle; *'Junior had suffered from a niggling thigh injury during the week and we had to decide whether to risk him and put him on later in the game if we needed him.*

'When he knew he would be starting on the bench, he said that Lee Thorpe could go out and do all the running around for 75 minutes and that he would come on at the end and score the winner. It's exactly how it turned out!'

Osman and Broadhurst would preside over one more game, at Bury on April 24th before they handed over the managerial reins to Ian Atkins, with Broadhurst staying on as his assistant.

That game ended in a goalless draw and there would be an emotional handing over to the new man at the last home game of the season, when Lincoln City were the visitors to the Memorial Stadium.

Rovers: Miller, Edwards, Anderson (J), Barrett, Austin, Gibb, Lescott, Hyde (Quinn), Anderson (I), Thorpe (Tait), Henriksen (Agogo).

Substitutes: Twigg, Clarke

Atkins Arrives

On Monday April 26th 2004 Rovers unveiled Ian Atkins as their new manager, though his appointment was hardly a surprise as it had been the worst kept secret in football.

His former club, Oxford United, had appointed Graham Rix as their new manager, paving the way for him to move him into the hot seat at the Memorial Stadium.

The former Birmingham, Everton and Sunderland defender had been in charge at Northampton Town prior to his move to Oxford United and had presided over Rover's play off semi-final defeat at the hands of the Cobblers back in 1998.

At the press conference to confirm his appointment, the new manager said; *'The situation here is similar to that at Northampton and Oxford, in that I'm taking on a club that has been struggling.*

'I know there will be massive expectation and that the fans have had it tough, but people are going to have to be patient. It's not a case of spending loads of money and waving a magic wand and there will be no quick fix.

'If we turn things around quickly and get where we want to go next season that will be a bonus. But it's going to take time and it will probably need two years just to sort the thing out.

'There's one major difference between Rovers and my last two clubs. At Northampton and Oxford they wanted everything by yesterday and there was constant pressure for results and big gates to break even.

'At Oxford it only took me a few months to realise that I had to keep winning to stay in the job. Here, I'm being given time to do the job properly and I'm able to plan for the long term future.'

On May 1st 2004 a crowd of 8,562 turned up to see the first game under Atkins and they saw Rovers register a 3-1 win against Lincoln City.

Paul Tait's 11th goal of the season, after just seven minutes, set the ball rolling. The striker picked up on a loose ball after goalkeeper Andy Marriott had only been able to parry Gary Twigg's shot, and he sidefooted in from close range.

Marcus Richardson beat Kevin Miller for the equaliser after 24 minutes, and it was all square at half time.

However, Tait scored again on 64 minutes when he picked up Lee Thorpe's through ball and beat Marriott with a fierce drive.

Ten minutes from time he nodded the ball into the path of his strike partner Thorpe, who was playing against one of his former clubs, and he more or less toe poked the ball over the line for his first Rovers goal.

Broadhurst, Atkins and Osman are pictured posing for photos at the end of the game, as one traumatic chapter closed and a new one began.

Rovers: Miller, Quinn, Edwards, Anderson (J), Barrett, Gibb, Williams (D), Lescott, Twigg (Agogo), Thorpe (Parker), Tait.

Substitutes: Williams (R), Haldane, Henriksen

The Summer Of 2004

The summer of 2004 proved to be a hectic one for Rovers and their supporters.

New manager Ian Atkins completely revamped his squad, bringing in a number of new faces, and there was a pre-season tour to the Isle of Man to take part in a week long, six team tournament with Carlisle United, Wrexham, Port Vale, Rushden & Diamonds and an island side.

Rovers were beaten by Rushden & Diamonds, on penalties, in the final but Atkins had been reluctant to see his side have such a tough week, playing competitive games against three league clubs.

'If it had been up to me, we wouldn't have gone, but it was something I inherited and supporters had already made bookings.

'It won't be on the agenda next year, but we made the most of it. Results in these games don't really mean anything. It's all about keeping the players fit, giving them the chance to play alongside each other and getting ready for the first game of the season at Mansfield.'

Prior to leaving for the Isle of Man, Rovers played a friendly against Bath City, at Twerton Park, when a crowd of 1,778 witnessed a goalless draw.

Taking part in that game were two German triallists, Thorsten Dinkel and Bernd Gagstatter, while a 15 year old Scott Sinclair made a brief cameo appearance.

Those three didn't go on tour, but two other players who were to enjoy the briefest of Rovers careers, did, namely Liam Burns and Jon Beswetherick.

The squad that Atkins had assembled for the start of his first season in charge bore little resemblance to the one that had completed the previous campaign and the new faces included Craig Hinton, Robbie Ryan, Paul Trollope, Steve Elliott, Stuart Campbell, James Hunt, Jamie Forrester, Craig Disley and Richard Walker.

The new season opened with a game against Mansfield Town, at Field Mill, on August 7th 2004 when two Junior Agogo goals gave Rovers a 2-0 win.

On a sweltering hot summers day Atkins handed full debuts to six players, while two more made their first appearance for the club when going on as substitutes.

However, it was one of the old guard, in the shape of Agogo (pictured), who caused the home side problems.

He opened the scoring on 31 minutes when he met Ali Gibb's cross from the right and struck a smart volley past home goalkeeper Kevin Pilkington.

The same combination linked up again seven minutes into the second half with Agogo finishing from close range following another ball into the box by Gibb.

Commenting after the game, Atkins said; *'I felt we always looked dangerous on the break and even though we allowed Mansfield a lot of possession in their own half, they didn't do a lot with it and I think they ran out of ideas a bit.'*

Rovers: Miller, Hinton, Edwards, Anderson, Ryan, Gibb, Hunt, Campbell (Elliott), Trollope, Forrester (Savage), Agogo (Walker).

Substitutes: Williams, Thorpe

A First For 'Swanny'

Following their opening day win at Mansfield, Rovers were held to a 2-2 draw by Bury at the Memorial Stadium just four days later.

It was a match that saw Rovers new striker Jamie Forrester score one penalty and have another saved by Bury goalkeeper Glyn Garner, in front of a crowd of 8,705.

Nevertheless, he was keen to remain the club's penalty taker, saying; *'All penalties are a game of bluff really.*

'I was very confident and, having scored one, I obviously wanted to take the second as well. Unfortunately for me, the keeper guessed the right way.

'I struck the ball well and I thought it was a good save. I've been taking penalties for a few seasons now and I'm confident about taking more and have no problem with it.'

Forrester retained his place in the side for Notts County's visit to the Memorial Stadium a few days later, on August 24th 2004, and was able to help the side celebrate their first home win of the season as the Magpies were beaten 2-1.

County, with future Rovers players David Pipe and Matt Gill in their lineup, and Steve Mildenhall on the bench, posed the bigger threat in a goalless first half but fell behind on 62 minutes when Christian Edwards scored his first goal in three and a half years.

The central defender was first to react when Stuart Campbell's corner arrived in the box and headed past goalkeeper Wayne Henderson from six yards.

Rovers were in front for just three minutes as Paul Bolland's cross found Glynn Hurst in space and he headed past Kevin Miller from inside the six yard box.

With nine minutes remaining, though, Junior Agogo ran on to Campbell's through ball and beat Henderson to score what proved to be the winning goal.

Goalscorer Edwards, who had last found the back of the net, for Nottingham Forest in March 2001, was surprised to open his Rovers account in this game; *'We had worked on set pieces in the week, although I had been used as a decoy rather than the target man.*

'But Stuart Campbell's delivery was so good that I managed to get a head on it and the next thing, it was in the back of the net.

'I've taken a bit of stick because Adam Barrett scored a few last season and John Anderson scored against Bury in midweek. I've never been prolific and three or four a season is as many as I've ever got.

'I was disappointed not to weigh in with one or two last season because I was having a competition with Adam.'

Instantly recognisable because of his height and his shoulder length hair, 'Swanny' (pictured about to celebrate) had to endure this quip from his manager; *'He won't have seen it go in, as his hair was in his eyes!'*

Rovers: Miller, Edwards, Anderson, Elliott, Gibb (Hinton), Ryan, Hunt, Trollope, Campbell (Savage), Forrester (Thorpe), Agogo.

Substitutes: Walker, Haldane.

Shrimpers Sunk

Three days after dumping Brighton & Hove Albion out of the League (Carling) Cup, Rovers entertained Southend United on Friday August 27th at the Memorial Stadium.

It was the first of four encounters against the Shrimpers that season, and the only occasion that Rovers would come out on top. As well as the two league meetings, the sides faced each other in the Area Final of the LDV Vans Trophy.

In the build up to this game, it was revealed that midfielder Dave Savage had handed in a transfer request, citing family reasons for his decision to move on; *'I'm not doing this to move to a bigger club because there isn't a bigger one than Bristol Rovers in this division.*

'It's simply that I have two daughters, aged three and eight and my wife is finding it hard bringing them up on her own because I am away such a lot.'

The week also saw the return of Aaron Lescott to the club. The defender had spent time on loan with Rovers during the previous season but had to negotiate his release from Stockport County before being able to sign for another club. He arrived, initially, on a six month deal with a view to extending it at some point in the future.

A Memorial Stadium crowd of 9,287 paid a moving tribute to former player and long serving groundsman Jackie Pitt before the game and then saw Rovers take a 13th minute lead through Lee Thorpe (pictured scoring), who applied the final touch to a Paul Trollope corner after Steve Elliott had managed the first.

Rovers held their lead until the 71st minute when their former skipper, Adam Barrett, equalised for the visitors when he glanced a header past goalkeeper Kevin Miller from Duncan Jupp's cross.

With four minutes remaining, Rovers scored the winner after Junior Agogo set Ali Gibb free down the right and his cross was met by James Hunt, who volleyed past Bart Griemink.

The three points sent Rovers to the top of the table for the first and only time that season, and manager Ian Atkins labelled the win as fantastic.

'If anyone had told me that we would be in this position after five league games I would have been delighted, especially to have the gap we have on some of the other teams I think will be there or thereabouts at the end of the season.

'There's an awful long way to go yet and things can still improve, but it's been a fantastic start.

'To win five and draw one at the start of the season, including knocking a Championship side out of the Carling Cup, is something special.

'There are things we need to do better, but these lads have only been together for two months so I can't complain too much.'

Rovers: Miller, Hinton, Edwards, Elliott, Ryan, Gibb (Savage), Hunt, Trollope, Campbell (Anderson), Agogo, Thorpe (Forrester).

Substitutes: Disley, Haldane.

First Defeat for Atkins

Manager Ian Atkins could hardly have made a better start to his time in charge at the Memorial Stadium.

When Rovers travelled to play Leyton Orient on September 11th, they did so with an eight game unbeaten run behind them.

However, that run was ended as Orient won 4-2 and things were never quite the same for the manager afterwards and his side went on to become the division's draw specialists, notching up a club record 22 games in which the points were shared come the end of the season.

Rovers began brightly at Brisbane Road and took the lead after 28 minutes when Kevin Miller's long clearance found Jamie Forrester (pictured) and he sprinted away from defender Alan White before beating goalkeeper Lee Harrison with a left foot shot.

The home side were back on level terms six minutes later when Michael Simpson headed past Miller from Lee Steele's cross.

Rovers regained the lead eight minutes into the second half thanks to Paul Trollope, who scored his first goal in a Rovers shirt when he collected a clearance from Harrison and hit a shot past the keeper from 15 yards which went in off the underside of the crossbar.

The home side hit back, though, and with former Rovers player Wayne Carlisle causing them problems out on the right, the home side equalised on 63 minutes through Steele who scored from close range following Andy Scott's ball into the box.

A minute later they were ahead as Carlisle's cross took a deflection off Christian Edwards and fell into the path of Gary Alexander, who comfortably beat Miller from close range.

Six minutes later Alexander scored again, nodding the ball past Miller from another Carlisle cross.

After the game Trollope who, a few years later, would lead the side to promotion, said; *'It was nice to get my first goal and shortly afterwards Lee (Thorpe) had a chance which could have put us 3-1 ahead.*

'If that had gone in the outcome might have been different. We've conceded a few goals now, straight after we've scored, which is disappointing and something we need to address.

'On another day we could have been comfortably in the lead before our bad patch at the end. After their two quick goals we were poor and a shadow of the team we had looked earlier.'

The manager wasn't impressed after seeing his side squander a number of chances and then throw away the lead through some poor defending; *'We should have been way out of sight after an hour. We hit the bar twice, had good chances, and could have scored six.*

'But over the last 25 minutes we stopped defending properly, especially dealing with balls at the back post. That annoyed me because we had spent three days working on balls being whipped in there.'

Rovers: Miller, Hinton, Edwards, Elliott, Ryan, Gibb, Hunt, Trollope (Agogo), Campbell (Disley), Thorpe, (Walker), Forrester.

Substitutes: Anderson, Lescott

Junior at the Double

A midweek win against Kidderminster Harriers in the first round of the LDV Vans Trophy was quickly followed, on October 2nd 2004, with a home league game against Oxford United.

It was a game that saw Rovers boss Ian Atkins face his former employers for the first time since a public falling out with the U's Chairman Firoz Kassam before his move to the Memorial Stadium.

'I don't give a monkey's that we are playing Oxford,' said Atkins, before adding *'I just want to get the three points. I always want a result, and this is no different.*

'If there are some sad people down there who try to stir it up, then that's up to them.'

He wasn't the only one to be facing his former club as striker Richard Walker and midfielder Dave Savage had previously turned out for the U' while former Rovers loanee Robert Wolleaston was in the Oxford squad.

Junior Agogo (pictured) scored the two goals that gave Rovers a comfortable win and saw them move up to fourth place in the table.

The in form striker first struck in the 44th minute when he was played in by Stuart Campbell and hit a shot into the corner of the net beyond goalkeeper Chris Tardiff.

His second arrived with eight minutes of the game remaining when he closed down the Oxford keeper as he was attempting to clear, and the ball fell for him to volley into an open goal from a narrow angle.

Those of you at that game might well recall one of the funniest incidents witnessed on the pitch during the time Atkins was manager at the club.

The manager was watching the game from the gantry in the West Stand and wasn't happy with the way Agogo was playing, so he phoned his assistant Kevan Broadhurst, who was on the bench, to ask for a message to be relayed to his striker while there was a break in play as an injured player was treated.

Broadhurst simply handed the phone to a very surprised Agogo who was told, in no uncertain terms, to put himself about a bit more!

The unusual kick up the backside obviously worked, and Atkins said this about the incident after the game; *'I got Kevan on the phone and asked him when he was going to get Junior going.*

'He said 'why don't you speak to him yourself' and put him on.

'It's probably against the rules, but the game had stopped, and he was off the pitch. I told him to move his arse, start making some runs and putting their defenders under pressure.

'Junior is a fantastic talent, but he really frustrates me at times. If only he worked a bit harder, he would score even more goals.'

Rovers: Miller, Edwards, Anderson, Elliott, Gibb, Savage, Lescott, Campbell (Hinton), Ryan, Thorpe, Agogo.

Substitutes: Forrester, Walker, Williams, Trollope

Cup Defeat at Carrow Road

Having been handed an away tie against Norwich City, in the Coca Cola Cup, Rovers took to the air to make their way to Carrow Road on September 21st 2004.

A 189 seat Boeing 737-800 carrying the team and supporters (pictured) who had paid £185 for the privilege of joining them, took off from Bristol airport for the 40 minute flight to Norfolk.

As they took off, there was a spontaneous chorus of 'The Gas are going up' from those on board. That was enjoyed by everyone apart from defender Christian Edwards, whose fear of flying saw him spend the whole time in the air with his head in his hands!

A crowd of 18,658 saw the home side go through to the next round of the competition thanks to Youssef Safri's goal in first half stoppage time.

The Moroccan hit a 30 yard shot past Kevin Miller to settle the tie and although Rovers had chances to get back on level terms after the break they were unable to beat home goalkeeper Robert Green.

They were reduced to ten men for the final minutes of the game when defender Steve Elliott was sent off after picking up his second yellow card of the night.

The game marked the only appearance of John Beswetherick's Rovers career. He had previously played for Plymouth Argyle and Sheffield Wednesday, and on leaving the Memorial Stadium he continued to play football, though left Paulton Rovers some time during the 2008/09 season because his work as a policeman meant that he was unable to commit to the club on a regular basis.

Jamie Forrester, who was left on the bench for the game, was looking forward to reclaiming his place in the side following the cup exit; *'I've said before that I would like to play in every game, but if I had to pick one out of the two I'd much rather play in our next league game than against Norwich in the League Cup.*

'We played only one up front against the Canaries and when that happens, I don't expect to be the first name on the teamsheet. If it's two or three up front I know I have more chance of playing.

'We were encouraged by the performance at Carrow Road, despite losing. We kept the ball really well at times and were a bit unlucky not to score.'

Rovers tried, without success, to get Elliott's red card rescinded; *'We had hoped that the referee would use some common sense given the circumstances,'* said manager Ian Atkins.

He went on to say; *'I didn't even think Steve deserved his first caution but the second was ridiculous and even the Norwich player asked the ref not to show another card, but to no avail.'*

Rovers: Miller, Hinton, Edwards, Anderson, Elliott, Gibb, Campbell (Walker), Hunt, Trollope (Lescott), Beswetherick (Disley), Agogo.

Substitutes: Thorpe, Forrester

Nine Men Earn A Point

Rovers entertained local rivals Yeovil Town on October 19th 2004 and manager Ian Atkins promised that his side would be fired up for the game, saying; *'It's probably our biggest game of the season.'*

What he didn't say was that he had 'previous' with Yeovil boss Gary Johnson. The two had fallen out way back in 1992, at Cambridge United. The U's sacked manager John Beck in October of that year and placed youth team boss Johnson in charge on a temporary basis.

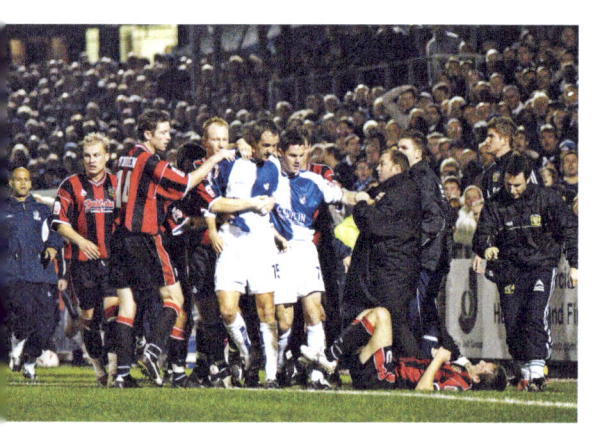

Seven games and six points later they installed Atkins as manager but kept Johnson in charge of the youth set up.

When he left the club after only five months in charge, Atkins had said; *'I wasn't being allowed to manage.'* And although he didn't go into detail, the fact that Johnson succeeded him as boss at the Abbey Stadium seemed to suggest that the two fell out big time.

He went on to say this about Johnson; *'We've come across each other a few times before and he's not on my Christmas card list after what he did to me at Cambridge, but that's life!'*

If there was ill feeling between the managers, it turned out to be none too friendly on the pitch, as Rovers had two players, Dave Savage and Steve Elliott, sent off in the first half.

Yeovil took the lead on 27 minutes when Paul Terry fired in a shot that took a deflection off a Rovers defender on its way past Kevin Miller and into the net.

Stoppage time saw referee Phil Crossley brandish two red cards. The first was to Savage (pictured being restrained by Stuart Campbell), who appeared to clip Gavin Williams (a future Rovers player) round the back of the head, the second to Elliott for allegedly aiming an elbow to the face of Phil Jevons.

Williams added a second goal for the visitors after 57 minutes, scoring from 15 yards with a left foot shot.

Rovers were then stung into action and when Junior Agogo found James Hunt in the area he turned the ball past Chris Weale to reduce the deficit. Incredibly, Rovers equalised with four minutes to go when Agogo picked up a loose ball inside the area and drilled a shot past Weale to end a remarkable night's football.

Following the game, Atkins was charged by the FA on three counts; that he used abusive and/or insulting language to Yeovil players in the tunnel at half time. That he did the same to Johnson at the end of the game and that he had to be physically restrained from confronting the Yeovil boss.

'My initial reaction is one of disbelief,' said the manager before adding *'but I won't be commenting publicly until I have answered these charges.'*

The fact that the game marked goalkeeper Kevin Miller's 600th league appearance was rather overshadowed by events that night!

Rovers: Miller, Edwards, Anderson, Elliott, Gibb (Campbell), Lescott (Thorpe), Hunt, Savage, Ryan, Walker (Hinton), Agogo.

Substitutes: Forrester, Disley

Swans on the Spot

A Wednesday night 2-0 win against Barnet in the second round of the LDV Vans Trophy was quickly followed by a league game against Swansea City at the Vetch Field, on November 6th 2004.

While both clubs had talked about moving into new, purpose built, stadia for as long as their supporters could remember, for the hosts it was about to become a reality.

The Swans were nine months shy of moving into a brand new stadium on the site of the former Morfa Athletic stadium.

This, therefore, was the last time that Rovers would play in the dilapidated ground known as the Vetch. It was to take Rovers another ten years to achieve their dream of receiving planning permission to build a new ground and as of 2022, they were still playing at the Memorial Stadium.

Rovers' final appearance in the crumbling old ground next to Swansea prison ended in defeat, the only goal of the game, a penalty, being scored three minutes from time.

Robbie Ryan was adjudged to have fouled Lee Trundle in the box as he lunged in trying to clear the ball. Trundle took the spot kick himself and Kevin Miller dived to his left to block the ball and sent it up over the bar.

However, the assistant referee ruled that the keeper had stepped forward before making the save and a retake was ordered. This time Trundle made no mistake from 12 yards and placed his effort just inside the post beyond Miller's reach.

The custodian wasn't happy with the decision to award a penalty in the first place, let alone the decision to have it retaken; *'It definitely wasn't a penalty because Robbie made a decent tackle and got a touch on the ball.*

'The referee was probably 20 yards behind him to his left and the linesman would have had the best view. I asked the ref to go over and ask the linesman what he thought, but he said he'd given the decision.

'When I made the save it was justice, but the referee did just about everything but put the ball in the net himself. As for the retake, the linesman said I moved three yards off my line when I made my save, but I don't go that far on my holidays!

'First the referee said there were players encroaching on the edge of the box, then he told me I'd moved off my line.

'I'm probably two yards off my line when I finish the save, but that's because I'm moving forward as Trundle is striking the ball.

'We saw it again in slow motion afterwards and even then, you can't tell so I don't know how he can make a decision like that in normal time.

'It would be nice if he (the referee) *would come out and apologise.'*

The photo shows Rovers midfielder James Hunt easing past Swansea's Roberto Martinez

Rovers: Miller, Edwards, Hinton, Burns, Ryan, Campbell (Gibb), Hunt, Lescott, Trollope (Walker), Agogo (Forrester), Thorpe.

Substitutes: Disley, Savage.

Two Against Wycombe

Rovers played seven games in November 2004, including two FA Cup ties against Carlisle United.

They ended the month with two games against Wycombe Wanderers, a league game at Adams Park, then known as the Causeway Stadium and an LDV Trophy Area Quarter Final at the Memorial Stadium.

The away game in the league came after a comprehensive home defeat at the hands of Scunthorpe United and defeat in an FA Cup replay at Carlisle.

They made it a hat trick against the Chairboys, slipping to a 1-0 defeat in front of a crowd of 4,999 on November 27th.

The only goal of the game came in the 54th minute, from the penalty spot after Nathan Tyson went to ground as he tried to get past Christian Edwards (pictured). Tyson picked himself up and beat Kevin Miller with his spot kick.

Manager Ian Atkins was none too happy with the penalty award and told reporters afterwards; *'The referee was conned, there was no contact whatsoever.*

'It's the second time in a couple of weeks we've been done by a dodgy penalty, and those decisions cost us games.'

Tyson, not surprisingly, saw things differently; *'He definitely made contact. I checked to come inside, and he clipped my ankle.*

'I've been through a barren spell recently so it's good to be scoring again. But I don't care whether I end up with 25 goals this season or not, as long as we go up.'

Wycombe's caretaker boss Keith Ryan sided with his striker; *'Nathan's an honest lad and doesn't have it in him to dive. Nothing I've seen on the video contradicts that. Ian Atkins is entitled to his opinion.'*

The result left Rovers in 15th place in the league standings and Atkins questioned whether or not his players had it in them to push on; *'We are getting to the stage of the season where I have to look at things and ask whether the people we have are going to take us forward.*

'Some players who might think they are doing okay could find themselves on the list so I can generate the means to bring others in.

'That doesn't just apply to those I inherited but one or two I brought in, who have done okay but I think could have done better.

'The hard part is getting the timing right because if clubs don't come in for players there's not a lot I can do. But regardless of this result, I know the areas we need to strengthen.'

Rovers: Miller, Hinton, Edwards, Elliott, Ryan, Campbell (Williams), Hunt, Trollope (Forrester), Savage, Agogo (Haldane), Thorpe. Substitutes: Lescott, Walker

Three days later, in front of a Memorial Stadium crowd of 3,667, Rovers gained swift revenge, beating the Chairboys by the same 1-0 scoreline.

Atkins made three changes to his starting lineup, with Lescott, Disley and Forrester replacing Ryan, Trollope and Agogo and it was Forrester who scored the all important goal.

Best Of The Season

It was hoped that the LDV Vans Trophy win against Wycombe, would be a turning point in a campaign that was fast becoming a big disappointment.

Rovers went into their next game, a home match against Chester City, on December 7th in 15th place but only three points off the play off places.

That position improved dramatically with a 4-1 win against their visitors that moved them four places up the league table.

The opening goal came with only three minutes on the clock with a move started and finished by midfielder Craig Disley (pictured).

He found Jamie Forrester out on the left and his angled drive was parried by goalkeeper Wayne Brown as far as Disley, who had continued his run through the middle and he comfortably slotted the ball home from six yards to register his first Rovers goal.

Chester equalised with a goal out of the blue, after 28 minutes, when Kevin Ellison's shot from the edge of the area flew into the far corner of the net with goalkeeper Kevin Miller stranded.

Rovers regained the lead in first half stoppage time when Dave Savage picked out Forrester's run into the area. However, the striker was fouled by Brown, who earned a caution for his efforts, and Rovers were awarded a spot kick which Forrester slammed into the net.

Goal number three arrived on 70 minutes when Lee Thorpe sent a looping header, from Steve Elliott's free kick, past Brown.

Paul Trollope, on as a second half substitute for Stuart Campbell, completed the scoring three minutes later when he was on hand to rifle the ball home from close range following a cross from Savage.

The manager was delighted with another excellent performance and said; 'That had been coming. Some of our recent performances hadn't been that bad but we hadn't had any breaks. This time we made things happen and I thought our performance was probably the best at home this season.'

He was also pleased with his strike force of Forrester and Thorpe, who were keeping Junior Agogo out of the starting lineup.

'I have looked at a number of permutations up front but at the moment I think 'Thorpey' and Jamie is probably the best one.

'I thought they were both outstanding. Lee is probably the best header of a ball at the club and is important in both penalty boxes, while Jamie has got six goals now despite starting a lot of games on the bench himself.'

There was also praise for Disley; 'He made a big difference for us because of his ability to get forward and he has been given licence to get in front of the strikers at times.

'I was really pleased he got his first goal for us and I think he is easily capable of six or seven, if not more, this season.'

Rovers: Miller, Hinton, Edwards, Elliott, Lescott, Campbell (Trollope), Hunt, Disley, Savage, Forrester (Agogo), Thorpe.

Substitutes: Williams, Walker, Burns

Scott's Debut

As Rovers prepared to face Leyton Orient on Boxing Day 2004 it was announced that 82 year old Denis Dunford would be stepping down from the Board after 18 years as a Director.

It would have been fitting, therefore, if the side could have given him the perfect send off by taking all three points.

It wasn't to be, though, as a Christmas crowd of 8,414 witnessed a 1-1 draw, two penalties, a red card, and a debut for one of the talented youngsters on Rovers books.

The red card was first to arrive and it was brandished at Rovers defender Robbie Ryan, for handling on the goal line.

That led to the game's first penalty, duly despatched by former Rovers defender Matt Lockwood.

Still trailing at the break, Rovers were awarded a spot kick of their own six minutes into the second half when Junior Agogo's cross from the right struck Andrew Scott on the arm.

That penalty was converted by Jamie Forrester, who sent goalkeeper Lee Harrrison the wrong way from 12 yards.

The result left the side in 14th position, a spot they would occupy going into 2005.

The game marked the debut of 15 year old Scott Sinclair (pictured), who became the second youngest player ever to pull on a Rovers shirt when he replaced Junior Agogo in the closing minutes.

The youngster had been at Rovers since the age of seven and at 15 years 277 days he followed Ronnie Dix, who had been 15 years and 180 days old when he made his debut in 1928, into the club record book.

'He's quick, he scores goals with either foot and he dribbles past people for fun', said Centre of Excellence Manager Stuart Naughton.

'He has come up through the youth system here and the club has looked after him. Because of that, I think he feels a loyalty to us.

'It's fantastic for him to have a taste of life around the first team at the age of 15 and he will benefit greatly from the experience, but part of my job will be to make sure his feet stay on the ground.'

Scott had this to say about his debut; *'It was a really big buzz when I went on and I'm really grateful to the gaffer for giving me a chance.'*

Stuart didn't get a lot more time to work with him, though, as after just one more substitute appearance for Rovers the youngster was snapped up by Chelsea.

That was in July 2005 and while he was at Stamford Bridge he turned out on loan for Plymouth Argyle, Queens Park Rangers, Charlton Athletic, Crystal Palace, Birmingham City and Wigan Athletic. He joined Swansea City, in a permanent deal in 2010, and signed for Manchester City two years later. He was loaned out to West Bromwich Albion in August 2013 and has since played for Aston Villa, Glasgow Celtic and Preston North End

Rovers: Miller, Hinton, Edwards, Elliott, Ryan, Hunt, Trollope, Savage, Campbell (Gibb), Agogo (Sinclair), Forrester (Anderson).

Substitutes: Lines, Cash

First Win Of 2005

Following the Boxing Day draw against Leyton Orient, Rovers drew 1-1 at Cheltenham in their final game of 2004 and stumbled into 2005 with a defeat at the hands of Shrewsbury Town on New Year's Day.

That loss left them in 14th place, but the first home game of the year, on January 3rd, saw them record a 3-1 win against Northampton Town to move them two places up the table.

Rovers were forced into an early change as midfielder Dave Savage limped off after only three minutes, to be replaced by Junior Agogo.

It took them 39 minutes to break the deadlock when James Hunt met a cross from Ali Gibb and headed past Lee Harper.

Christian Edwards doubled the lead six minutes into the second half when Harper struggled to get to Gibb's corner and could only touch the ball as far as the Rovers central defender who fired home from ten yards.

Ryan Clarke made number of fine saves to keep the visitors at bay, but manager Ian Atkins felt comfortable enough to send on midfielder Brian Cash, for Jamie Forrester with 12 minutes remaining.

The visitors pulled a goal back through Eric Sabin who was on hand to net from close range when Trevor Benjamin's effort came back off the bar.

Eleven minutes after going on for his debut, Cash was himself replaced when Atkins sent on Elliott Ward (the two are pictured here; Cash is on the right).

Rovers put the game beyond all doubt on the 90 minute mark when Agogo beat Harper after exchanging passes with Lee Thorpe.

The talking point afterwards was the substitution of the substitute, but all Atkins would say was; *'I felt a bit sorry for him but at that stage of the game we needed a big centre half on because Northampton were bombarding us. I'm not here to massage anyone's ego, I'm here to win games of football.'*

Those 11 minutes turned out to be the only game time of Cash's brief Rovers career.

Reflecting on the game against his former club, the manager said; *'I don't think we've been dealt many good cards in recent weeks, but we got a few breaks.*

'We had to dig deep to beat a good Northampton side and we had limited options because of the people we were missing, so I think we can be proud of the players.'

There were connections between the clubs all over the pitch as Northampton fielded former Rovers player Josh Low in their starting lineup, along with Scott McGleish, a future Rovers player.

As well as the managerial connection, Rovers fielded four former Northampton players, in Savage, Hunt, Forrester and Gibb.

Savage, whose game lasted only three minutes because of a hamstring injury, was being linked with a move to Leyton Orient as Atkins came under pressure to reduce the wage bill at the Memorial Stadium.

Rovers: Clarke, Hinton, Edwards, Elliott, Ryan, Gibb, Hunt, Trollope, Savage (Agogo), Thorpe, Forrester (Cash), (Ward).

Substitutes: Walker, Haldane

A Share Of The Spoils Again

Sent off for making an abusive remark to his own bench at Lincoln City the previous week, Junior Agogo was to miss the game against Cheltenham Town on January 22nd 2005 due to suspension.

However, manager Ian Atkins was able to recall central defender John Anderson to the squad after he had served a three match ban and Ryan Williams, who was recalled from a loan spell with Forest Green Rovers.

In charge of Cheltenham was former Rovers boss John Ward and Atkins, aware that his side needed a win rather than a draw, realised it was going to be a tough game; *'We know Cheltenham will make it very hard for us to break them down. 'We have seen other teams do it and it can be very frustrating for our fans if we don't get the breakthrough early on.*

'I know we have had too many draws and some of our games have frustrated our fans, because they have frustrated me too. When teams have come here to try and play a bit of football, like Northampton and Chester, we have won well. But others have come here to put men behind the ball and hope for a break.'

After all that, he saw his side go out and record a seventh draw in nine games, watched by a crowd of 6,954 at a rain sodden Memorial Stadium.

Ward received a good reception from the home fans when he walked across the pitch at the start of the game and saw his side take a 38th minute lead thanks to a goal from future Rovers player Steven Gillespie.

When Brian Wilson's cross from the right eluded defender Craig Hinton, Gillespie found the space to get away a shot which hit Christian Edwards. That wrong footed goalkeeper Ryan Clarke before ending up in the back of the net.

The equaliser arrived deep into first half stoppage time and came courtesy of a mistake by former Rovers keeper Shane Higgs, who came out to smother an attempted Lee Thorpe shot. He couldn't hold on to the ball, though, allowing Thorpe (pictured) a second opportunity to shoot and he drilled the ball into an open goal.

There were no further goals, even though the visitors ended the match with ten men following a 76th minute red card for Grant McCann following an altercation with Stuart Campbell.

After the match Ward was asked about Gillespie, a former Bristol City striker, who was subjected to almost constant abuse throughout the afternoon; *'In spite of the abuse he scored a goal - did well, didn't he?*

'Whatever 'head' he is, it's alright by me and at the moment he's a 'Robinhead' I told him they were only words and weren't going to hurt him, but I also advised him to stay in tonight!'

Rovers: Clarke, Hinton, Edwards, Elliott, Ryan, Disley, Campbell, Hunt, Trollope (Williams), Thorpe, Forrester (Anderson).

Substitutes: Walker, Haldane, Lescott

Grimsby Sent Packing

In spite of a 3-2 defeat at the hands of his former club, Oxford United, Rovers boss Ian Atkins hadn't given up hope of his side reaching the end of season play offs.

'Of course we can still go up because this league is so wide open. But I'm not happy with our position and we need to start winning games soon if we are to challenge.'

Atkins was speaking ahead of the visit of Grimsby Town, on February 5th 2005, to the Memorial Stadium.

The manager was still looking to strengthen his squad and a few days before the game he had fielded four triallists in a reserve team game against Bournemouth, which ended in a 2-2 draw.

For the record, they were Chris McDonald (Southampton), Ahmed Rifat (Reading), Kyle Nix (Aston Villa) and Danny Bunt (West Ham). No, I've never heard of them since, either!

A crowd of 6,134 saw the game against Grimsby and Atkins was still banging on about the play offs on the morning of the game, presumably trying to motivate his players ahead of kick off; *'The gloves are off,'* he said, before adding; *'We can't keep talking about the play offs, we have to do something about getting there.'*

His side obviously took notice of his comments, as they took all three points that afternoon thanks to a 3-0 win.

All three goals arrived in the first half and it was James Hunt (pictured) who opened the scoring on 27 minutes when he latched on to a pass from Junior Agogo and drove a shot into the top corner of the net.

Eleven minutes later Ryan Williams, on for the injured Paul Trollope after only 18 minutes, doubled the lead when his sweetly struck left foot volley beat goalkeeper Tony Williams.

On the stroke of half time Richard Walker ran on to a long clearance and lifted a shot over Williams to give his side a comfortable lead which they defended well in the second half thanks, in no small part, to goalkeeper Ryan Clarke who made a number of impressive saves.

In fact, the young goalkeeper was awarded the Man of the Match accolade and his manager said; *'Ryan was tremendous and made a couple of great saves to keep us in it.*

'He had a little wobble at Oxford last week, but it's all new to him. He was always going to play in this game because Kevin Miller has only been back for a week following injury and wasn't quite ready.

'Ryan's judgement was spot on in very difficult conditions and he's done very well in a couple of one on ones. But then that's what he's there for and the defenders and midfielders deserve a lot of credit for trying to protect him.'

Rovers: Clarke, Lescott, Edwards, Elliott, Ryan, Campbell (Hinton), Hunt, Disley, Trollope (Williams), Walker, Agogo (Haldane).

Substitutes: Forrester, Lines

Humbled At Huish

Following the win against Grimsby Town, and in the build up to the game against Yeovil Town at Huish Park, manager Ian Atkins allowed striker Lee Thorpe to join Swansea City.

His departure gave another opportunity for Richard Walker to impress the manager, not long after he had been linked with a permanent move to Kidderminster Harriers and a loan move to Cambridge United.

Meanwhile Atkins was taking a look at Nigerian international Minabo Asechemie who was training with the club and hoping to feature in a reserve game against Cardiff (before you ask, I have no idea if that game went ahead, or what happened to Asechemie!).

A week is a long time in football, and although everyone was upbeat following the three goal victory against the Mariners, they were brought back to earth just seven days later when losing 4-2 against Yeovil.

Mysteriously, Atkins phoned in sick for this one and left assistant Kevan Broadhurst in charge. There was speculation that the 'gaffer' had ducked out of the game because of his spat with Yeovil boss Gary Johnson at the Memorial Stadium the previous October; how could they!

In front of a crowd of 9,153 down in Somerset, Rovers opened the scoring after 17 minutes. Aaron Lescott made a run down the right and found Junior Agogo who played the ball into the path of Craig Disley (both players are pictured here), and he drilled a 25 yard effort past home goalkeeper Chris Weale.

Rovers held the lead for eight minutes before Phil Jevons volleyed a 25 yard effort past Ryan Clarke.

Jevons struck again five minutes into the second half, this time from the penalty spot after Christian Edwards was adjudged to have handled. The striker sent Clarke the wrong way from 12 yards to put his side in front.

He went on to complete his hat trick just after the hour mark, when he scored from close range following Andy Lindegaard's cross.

Goal number four arrived on 71 minutes courtesy of Bartosz Tarachulski who met a cross from Arron Davies and beat Clarke with a looping header.

Although Walker pulled a goal back two minutes from time, Rovers were well beaten in front of 1,500 travelling Gasheads.

After the match Broadhurst revealed that Atkins missed the game due to bronchitis, saying; *'Ian's been ill for about four weeks now and we've had a lot of flu and illness in the camp.*

'It turns out he's got bronchitis, he's not very well at all.'

The assistant manager was also concerned with a growing injury list; *'We could be down to 12 fit professionals for the visit of Southend in the LDV Vans Trophy game on Tuesday and five of those are strikers.'*

Rovers: Clarke, Lescott, Edwards (Williams), Hinton, Ryan, Campbell (Haldane), Hunt, Disley, Trollope, Agogo, Walker.

Substitutes: Forrester, Lines, Sinclair

Eight Goals Shared

After defeat against Yeovil Town in February, Rovers lost the first leg of the Area Final of the LDV Vans Trophy, beaten 2-1 by Southend United at the Memorial Stadium.

They followed that up with a run of six games in which they lost only once. Trouble is, the other five all ended in draws!

One of those was the second leg of the LDV Area Final, so Southend went through to the final, winning 3-2 on aggregate.

Following a record breaking 18th draw of the season at Bury, on March 12th, manager Ian Atkins decided to hand the goalkeeper's jersey to Ryan Clarke for the remaining nine games of the season, saying; *'Kevin's (Miller) contract is up at the end of the season and now he's 36 I don't know whether he wants to carry on playing or go into coaching.'*

The manager was taking a look at former Birmingham City and Hartlepool United defender Jon Bass in the lead up to the game against Mansfield Town on March 19th, while he was also reported to be interested in signing Accrington Stanley midfielder Rory Prendergast.

Rovers were unable to register a first win since February 5th, though, and had to be content with another draw, albeit one in which eight goals were shared!

Richie Barker gave the Stags a 19th minute lead, after Clarke could only block Scott McNiven's shot, allowing Barker to net from close range.

Two minutes later Ryan Williams, one of two former Mansfield players in the squad (Craig Disley being the other) levelled when he cut in from the left and drilled a shot past goalkeeper Kevin Pilkington.

Richard Walker scored a 45th minute penalty, after Lewis Haldane had been brought down by McNiven, to give Rovers a half time lead.

A minute into the second half Colin Larkin fired past Clarke to level the scores and Barker edged the Stags in front when he headed home from a Fraser McLachlan cross.

Calum Lloyd increased the lead after 68 minutes, with another close range effort.

Rovers hit back, though, and Junior Agogo scored from Rovers' second penalty of the game, awarded after Jake Buxton had tugged at his shirt in the area.

Then, with two minutes of the game remaining Pilkington, under pressure from Disley (pictured) failed to hold on to Steve Elliott's ball into the box and Jamie Forrester pounced to net a dramatic equaliser.

Although he praised his side for the way they fought back from 4-2 down, Atkins was not a happy man at the final whistle; *'The game was riddled with mistakes and after getting our noses in front we made two horrendous errors at the start of the second half.*

'The goals we gave away were very poor, although the pitch isn't the best at the moment and had a lot to do with a couple of them.'

Rovers: Clarke, Hinton (Disley), Anderson, Elliott, Ryan, Hunt, Lescott, Williams, Haldane (Forrester), Walker, Agogo.

Substitutes: Trollope, Edwards, Miller

At Last…A Win On The Road!

In the build up to the game against Notts County, at Meadow Lane, on March 26th 2005 Rovers signed Chris Carruthers on loan until the end of the season.

The former England Youth international arrived at the Memorial Stadium from Northampton Town, thus swelling the ranks of the former Cobblers players at the club.

Carruthers found himself on the bench for the trip to Nottingham and by the time he entered the fray, in the 78th minute, his new side were 2-1 ahead, a lead they kept to take all three points.

It was their first away win in seven months and they had to come from behind to record a victory that left them in 17th place in the League Two standings.

Glyn Hurst opened the scoring for the home side on eight minutes, after goalkeeper Ryan Clarke had parried a shot from Stefan Oakes straight to the Magpies midfielder who scored from close range.

The equaliser arrived a minute before half time when Robbie Ryan drove a low ball into the area where Junior Agogo (pictured) scored his 20th goal of the season when he knocked the ball in from a yard out.

Eight minutes into the second half Richard Walker scored what proved to be the winning goal when he met a cross from Aaron Lescott and headed the ball over goalkeeper Robert Elliott for his ninth goal of the campaign.

Lescott and Walker were both former Aston Villa trainees and used to travel down to Bristol together every day, with Lescott doing all of the driving as Walker had never taken his driving test. After the match, therefore, the striker quipped that he would have a job to stop his team mate banging on about the quality of the cross that enabled him to score.

'I'll be hearing about it all the way home, and for several weeks to come. Aaron will be in my ear, have no doubt about that. Perhaps I'll just remind him of the few chances he had in the game that he missed!'

He was, though, delighted to have been on the scoresheet; *'I didn't expect a free header but luckily I saw the keeper off his line and just tried to get the ball over him.*

'That away win has been a long time coming and the boys are absolutely buzzing in the dressing room. If only we could have done this earlier in the season, who knows what might have happened?'

He was relishing the opportunity of a regular place in the starting lineup; *'It's just nice to be getting a run in the side and nice to be scoring a few goals as well, because that really helps your confidence. Now I want to try and reach double figures before the end of the season.'*

Rovers: Clarke, Hinton, Anderson, Elliott (Edwards), Lescott, Hunt, Disley, Savage, (Carruthers), Ryan, Agogo (Haldane), Walker.

Substitutes: Williams, Forrester

Another High Scoring Draw

It was the season of draws as far as Rovers were concerned and another one came along on March 28th 2005 when they shared six goals with Darlington.

The game came just two days after the away win against Notts County and extended the unbeaten run to six, although this was the fifth draw in that sequence.

Rovers gained a point the hard way, coming back from two goals down to salvage something It was the fourth time that season they had achieved the feat.

They fell behind with only 54 seconds on the clock and it stemmed from a long clearance by goalkeeper Sam Russell. The ball reached Chris Hughes, who played it on to Russell who fired home in spite of a valiant attempt by Ryan Clarke to prevent the ball crossing the line.

Rovers struggled to make an impact in the opening half but conjured up an equaliser on the stroke of half time when Junior Agogo's shot was blocked and the rebound fell to Richard Walker who scored with a left foot volley.

Darlington were awarded a penalty five minutes into the second half when Aaron Lescott's challenge on Jason St'Juste in the area was deemed to be an unfair one and Craig Hignett sent Clarke the wrong way from 12 yards.

The visitors extended their lead just after the hour mark when St'Juste made a determined run from the halfway line and beat Clarke with a shot from 15 yards.

The goal seemed to sting Rovers into action and Steve Elliott pulled a goal back on 69 minutes, heading home following a Ryan Williams corner.

Two minutes later they were back on level terms when Williams was again the provider, this time finding Walker (pictured) who shot past Russell from 14 yards.

Speaking afterwards Walker, whose two goals took him into double figures for the season, and earned his side their 20th draw of the campaign, said; *'At the moment I feel as though I can score in every game and when you are on a run like that, you don't think anyone can stop you.*

'If I can get a few more goals before the end of the season, it means my confidence will stay high over the summer and, hopefully, will get me off to a good start next time.'

Manager Ian Atkins, meanwhile, informed the press that he felt that midfielder Craig Disley needed to 'beef up' during the summer months. He had previously stated that the player was anaemic and given him a bottle of vitamin tablets!

'He is one of the players we really need to look to and examine how they live so we can strengthen him up.

'If there's one area of his game we need to improve it's his determination, not so much on the ball as off it.'

Rovers: Clarke, Hinton (Williams), Anderson, Elliott, Lescott, Hunt (Edwards), Savage, Ryan, Disley (Forrester), Agogo, Walker.

Substitutes: Haldane, Carruthers

Diamond Geezers!

On April 9th 2005, Rovers recorded their first home win for two months when they comfortably beat Rushden & Diamonds 3-0.

The build up to the game was more about the pink shirts that had been unveiled as part of an elaborate April Fool's joke.

The club had run a story on their official website saying that they planned to introduce a pink shirt as the third kit the following season, and fans signed an online petition to make it happen, with several of them pledging to buy one.

As a result, the club agreed to have a limited number of pink shirts produced by their kit suppliers, Errea. There was a later agreement that the side would play a pre-season friendly in their fetching pink strip and that for every shirt purchased £4 would be donated to Cancer Research UK's 'Think Pink' cancer awareness campaign.

As for the game against Rushden, the Memorial Stadium crowd of 5,740 saw Rovers take a first half lead through Richard Walker (pictured celebrating) after 22 minutes.

The striker took possession some 30 yards out and raced towards goal before beating goalkeeper Scott Shearer with a shot that entered the net off the far post.

The lead was doubled just before the hour mark when Craig Disley headed the ball against the crossbar from a corner and was quick enough to pick up the rebound and drive it into the net from 12 yards.

Shearer, who was on loan from Coventry was, of course, a future Rovers custodian. He made a number of crucial saves for the visitors but was left red faced with seven minutes remaining when, under pressure from Walker following a corner, he managed to palm the ball into his own net for goal number three.

Speaking after the game, Walker had this to say; 'We played ever so well. We closed down, worked hard and made it difficult for their full backs to get out.

'As for my goal, Craig Disley did well closing one of their players down and the ball reached me via a lucky ricochet. However, I was surprised to see I had so much space. I managed to take it on and slot it into the corner, so I was really pleased.'

The striker was also hoping to claim the third goal, even though it looked to be an own goal to most people in the crowd; 'I'm pretty sure I got a touch on it before it went over the line. The ref's given it to me so, hopefully, now I'll be credited with it.

'The keeper went up unopposed and just seemed to throw it back towards the goal and it was definitely a strange one. I was just happy to knock it in.'

Research, though, shows he had to be content with just the one goal that afternoon!

Rovers: Clarke, Edwards, Anderson, Elliott, Lescott, Savage, Disley, Ryan, Walker, Agogo, Williams (Sinclair).

Substitutes: Trollope, Lines, Forrester, Carruthers

Wycombe Wonders!

The title of this particular article says it all, because it wasn't only Wycombe wondering about Rovers' lineup, it was almost everyone else as well. Quite how he did it I don't know, but manager Ian Atkins managed to persuade the Football League that because of injuries and suspensions he was unable to field a side against the Chairboys.

This was in spite of the fact that when the game was played, on May 7th 2005 he was able to name a bench that included Paul Trollope, Jamie Forrester, Lewis Haldane and Chris Lines!

He must have been very persuasive, as the club was granted special dispensation to sign no fewer than three players for a meaningless final game of the season.

Consequently, Alex Jeannin and Jefferson Louis started the match and young Louie Soares was named on the bench with the aforementioned Rovers players.

As it was, a Memorial Stadium crowd of 7,358, witnessed a dire game which Rovers won courtesy of Richard Walker's 11th minute goal.

Played in by Chris Carruthers, Walker headed past goalkeeper Lance Cronin, a future Rovers goalkeeper, to seal the win. There was another future Rovers player, in the shape of Danny Senda in the Wycombe side, whose manager John Gorman couldn't believe Rovers had managed to sign three players for this one game.

Ryan Williams is pictured on the ball, with Jeannin behind him.

With almost as many players missing as the hosts, his reaction was as follows; 'My thoughts are unprintable! What rule is it that allows a manager to bring in three new players at this stage of the season? I certainly didn't know there was any such rule.

'You could see how the new lads gave Rovers a lift. I gave some of our younger players a chance to show what they could do, and they didn't take it.'

He wasn't happy with the pitch, either!

'It was awful, the worst I've ever seen down here. The pitch and the wind made this a nasty place to cone to. We wanted to finish on a high, but the circumstances did not allow us to do that.'

Atkins must have had his tongue planted firmly in his cheek at the post-match press conference, when he said; 'We were very fortunate that the three players were made available because, without them, we would not have had a team.

'I thought the new lads were fantastic for us. Coming in at such short notice must have been difficult for them and we only had half an hour on the training ground to work with them after they arrived.

'To start the game with two non-contract players, a loan signing (Carruthers) and a player who is on week to week contracts (Jon Bass) and beat a team of Wycombe's capabilities and capacity was incredible. It's probably our best result of the season.'

Team: Clarke, Edwards (Trollope), Anderson, Elliott, Bass, Jeannin, Lescott, Williams (Soares), Carruthers, Walker, Louis (Haldane).

Substitutes: Forrester, Lines

Some You May Have Forgotten

A glance through the list of those who turned out for the club in 2004/05 shows that manager Ian Atkins certainly had an eye for a player.

Three years later many of those he signed in the summer of 2004 were helping the club win promotion in a Wembley play off final against Shrewsbury Town.

Whilst most of the permanent signings he made were sound there were other, short term and loan deals, that didn't quite turn out as they might have.

Jon Beswetherick (pictured), Liam Burns, Brian Cash and Elliott Ward would almost certainly tell you that they weren't given a fair crack of the whip by the Rovers boss.

Beswetherick arrived at Rovers in the summer of 2004 with over 100 Plymouth Argyle league games to his name and experience of playing for Sheffield Wednesday, Swindon Town and Macclesfield Town.

However, he was to make just one first team appearance under Atkins, against Norwich City in the second round of the Coca Cola Cup at Carrow Road. He was on the bench for the next two league games and then he moved on to Kidderminster Harriers. He went on to play for Forest Green Rovers, Salisbury City, Mangotsfield United, Weston super Mare and Paulton Rovers before being released by them due to his work commitments as a police officer.

Burns had appeared in over 100 league games for Port Vale before pitching up at the Memorial Stadium. The Belfast born defender was marginally more successful that Beswetherick, as he did manage to make four first team appearances under Atkins. His stay, at the Memorial Stadium though, was almost as brief.

Short spells with Shrewsbury Town, Kidderminster Harriers and Forest Green Rovers followed before he returned to Ireland where he helped Sligo Rovers win the League of Ireland First Division title in 2005.

With Bohemians he was a League of Ireland Cup runner up in 2007 and was in the side that completed a League of Ireland and FAI Cup double in 2008.

He then played for Dundalk, returned to Bohemians and in 2012 moved to Dundalk for a second time.

The one, brief, appearance by Cash is covered elsewhere in this publication (Page 69). In the game in which he made his debut, Cash was replaced by a defender, Ward who had already made an appearance as a late substitute at Cheltenham, but in a wide midfield role!

The West Ham player had already been on loan at Peterborough United before he arrived at the Mem and after three sub appearances for us he moved to Plymouth, again on loan, before a permanent move to Coventry City in 2006.

He played on loan at Doncaster Rovers and Preston North End before joining Norwich City in 2010 and enjoyed two loan spells with Nottingham Forest in 2012/13 before signing for AFC Bournemouth, in 2013. He has since played for Huddersfield Town, Blackburn Rovers, MK Dons, Notts County and Cambridge United and ended the 2019/20 season with Chelmsford City.

Opening Day Point

Rovers kicked off the 2005/06 campaign on August 6th 2005 with a point from a 1-1 draw at Barnet, courtesy of a Junior Agogo goal.

Manager Ian Atkins was undecided on his starting lineup until the last minute, before opting not to include midfielder Matt Somner who had signed non-contract forms before setting off for Underhill.

He did, though, hand goalkeeper Scott Shearer his Rovers debut and included Jefferson Louis on the bench. The striker, who had appeared in the final game of the previous season, had signed a six month contract during the summer.

The home side, newly promoted from the Conference as champions, fielded a familiar face in attack in former Rovers striker Giuliano Grazioli, who is pictured here with Agogo and Louis.

Rovers' central defender John Anderson lasted just 11 minutes of the season's opener and had to leave the pitch with a broken nose but his side, kicking down the notorious Underhill slope, failed to capitalise on any advantage that might have given them and were under the cosh for much of the goalless first half.

It was a similar story after the break, and it was no surprise when Barnet edged in front with 14 minutes left when Shearer misjudged the flight of Ismail Yakubu's free kick. The ball fell to Richard Graham who hit a left foot shot into the net.

However, Rovers conjured up an unlikely equaliser with just three minutes of the game remaining. Ryan Williams picked out Junior Agogo with a curling cross, and he beat goalkeeper Scott Tynan with a close range header.

Barnet manager Paul Fairclough described the result as 'a 1-1 slaughter', while Atkins said; 'One long ball over the top gave them a goal. We didn't concentrate when we didn't have possession and gave the ball away too cheaply.

'As a performance, in terms of something to watch it was poor, but the first game of the season is always a difficult one, especially coming here for Barnet's first game back in the Football League.'

Williams, who had been on the verge of leaving the club the previous season and who had spent time on loan with Forest Green Rovers, was delighted with his contribution and the continuing support of the Rovers faithful; 'The fans have been absolutely brilliant to me and I'd love to do something to pay them back. Even when it looked like I might be leaving the club they got behind me and encouraged me. That's not the sort of thing you forget, and I can't thank them enough.'

The reason given for Somner's absence was given as a failure, by the FA, to register his forms and he said; 'I thought I was playing when I arrived at the ground and I went through my usual preparation and got myself pumped up.

'Then the gaffer read out the team and I knew my registration hadn't come through.'

Rovers: Shearer, Bass (Williams), Elliott, Anderson (Hinton), Edwards, Ryan, Disley, Lescott, Campbell, Agogo, Walker (Louis).

Substitutes: Forrester, Gibb

Back To Back Home Defeats

Following their draw at Underhill on the opening day of the season, Rovers suffered a home defeat at the hands of Grimsby Town three days later and when Peterborough United visited the Memorial Stadium on August 13th 2005, they slipped to their second home defeat of the week.

The visitors fielded two former Rovers loan players in Chris Plummer and James Quinn and made the best possible start, scoring after only five minutes when Quinn laid the ball off to Adam Newton who curled a shot into the net from the edge of the area.

They increased their lead after 23 minutes when Robbie Ryan's intended back pass to John Anderson was intercepted by Dave Farrell who went on to beat Scott Shearer with a shot from 20 yards. Ryan is pictured challenging for the ball, watched by Ryan Williams and Steve Elliott.

Peterborough were reduced to ten men after 38 minutes when their skipper, Dean Holden, appeared to stamp on Shearer as he gathered the ball.

Rovers took advantage of their numerical advantage as the half drew to a close and Richard Walker headed home from six yards, following James Hunt's cross, to reduce the arrears.

Having upped the tempo at the start of the second period, a deserved equaliser arrived on 57 minutes. Plummer was penalised for a foul some 25 yards from goal, and Steve Elliott stepped up to beat goalkeeper Mark Tyler with a fierce 25 yard free kick.

Rovers' joy was short lived, though, as the visitors stole all three points when Richard Logan scored their third goal following Peter Gain's cross from the right.

Manager Ian Atkins, who had lost his right hand man Kevan Broadhurst in the summer, appeared to be frustrated in his attempts to lift his side; *'I don't think people realise how frustrating it is as a manager when you know what you need to improve, but you can't get it.*

'Other clubs have got an assistant manager, a coach and a fitness coach, but I'm doing everything on my own here, including the scouting, so it's a one man band. But I'll get on with it.'

Three days after his rant to the press, Atkins was given some assistance, when the club announced that midfielder Paul Trollope was to be the new player/coach. He was delighted to be given the chance; *'Coaching has been an area I've wanted to progress into for a while now, so when this position became available it was obviously something I was very interested in.*

'You never know when opportunities in football are going to come along, and this is something I'm excited about and looking forward to. Hopefully, my appointment will help the manager out a bit.'

We didn't know it at the time, but Trollope's appointment was to have a great significance on the next chapter in the club's history.

Rovers: Shearer, Gibb, Edwards, Anderson (Hinton), Elliott, Ryan (Forrester), Campbell, Hunt, Williams, Agogo (Louis), Walker.

Substitutes: Somner, Disley

First Win Of The Season

Without a win to their name in their opening three games, Rovers travelled to Torquay on August 20th 2005 hoping to break their duck.

They almost never reached their destination, as the team coach broke down en route and the players had to wait by the roadside for a replacement vehicle to come from Torquay to transport them to the ground.

Then, in front of a Plainmoor crowd of 3,964, which included 1,521 Rovers fans, they managed to bring back the three points… just!

The home side took the lead on 21 minutes when Liam Coleman threaded the ball between defenders Steve Elliott and John Anderson to Leon Constantine, who hit a shot past Scott Shearer.

The Gulls took that lead into the half time break and added a second goal just before the hour mark when former Bristol City player Matt Hewlett forced the ball home from close range after Brian McGlinchey's cross from the right.

Still trailing by those two goals as the clocked ticked on to 74 minutes, Rovers at last sprang into action and Junior Agogo latched on to Richard Walker's through ball before beating goalkeeper Andy Marriott with a ferocious left foot drive.

With two minutes left, it seemed likely that the goal would be nothing more than a consolation.

However, Agogo was on fire and scored again when he accepted another pass from Walker and ran at the home defenders before beating Marriott with a stunning effort for the equaliser.

Rovers weren't finished, though, and deep into stoppage time the two goal hero fed his fellow striker Walker and he hit a right foot shot into the corner of the net for the winning goal.

Walker is pictured celebrating with Craig Disley and Ryan Williams.

Not surprisingly, manager Ian Atkins was encouraged by his side's performance; *'We didn't deserve to be two goals down, but the evidence was there again for all to see and just underlined what I've been saying for the past 10 months.*

'We can't keep coming back from two goals down every week because it's impossible, and we can't keep giving ourselves a mountain to climb if we are going to achieve.

'We've identified the area that needs strengthening, but unless I'm told I can bring people in then what can I do apart from continue to work with the players we have got?

'If we are to go forward, I have to be given the opportunity to bring people in and strengthen the team. People can shout and scream as much as they want, and some of the abuse I took from behind the dugout was a disgrace, but tell me what I can do about it.'

Paul Trollope was on the touchline in his player/coach capacity for the first time, and the midfielder was already making an impression with the players. The gaffer's time was running out!

Rovers: Shearer, Gibb (Williams), Ryan, Anderson, Elliott, Campbell (Disley), Lescott, Hunt, Hinton, Louis (Walker), Agogo.

Substitutes: Forrester, Bass

September's Winning Start

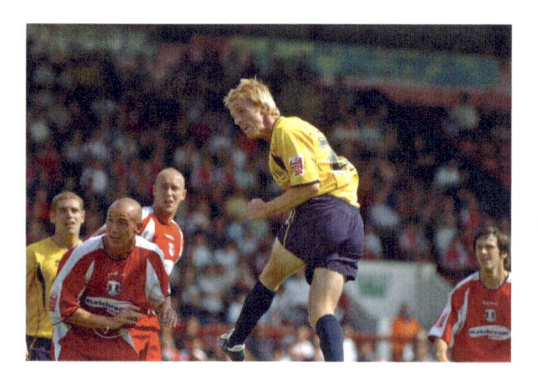

Ahead of the game against Leyton Orient at Brisbane Road on September 3rd 2005, manager Ian Atkins had been busy wheeling and dealing.

Popular winger Ryan Williams had been packed off to Aldershot on a month's loan, though the manager neglected to tell him he was on his way; *'To be placed on the list and not even know about it is a shock,'* said Williams.

'The manager obviously has his own methods, but I'm absolutely gutted and feel I've been treated harshly.

'I'm the kind of lad who trains every day and never complains, even when I'm not in the team. I'm upset by what has happened and I don't deserve to be treated like this.

'I knew nothing about going to Aldershot until my agent phoned me and told me last night. This is the final straw as far as I'm concerned.'

As Williams was on his way out, Michael Leary was on his way in, arriving from Luton Town also in a one month loan deal.

The midfielder, speaking before his debut at Brisbane Road, said; *'It's been so difficult to hold down a position at Luton, simply because the team has been so successful. There's no way the gaffer can possibly change the team in those circumstances.*

'Of course it's been frustrating but there's not a lot I can do about it without getting out there and actually playing.'

Rovers began the game against Orient, their fourth successive away game, in a positive fashion and took the lead through Craig Disley (pictured) after 15 minutes.

Leary fed Junior Agogo down the right and he, in turn, played the ball back to Ali Gibb who delivered a perfect left foot cross into the box where Disley powered a header past goalkeeper Glyn Garner.

Agogo scored the second goal from the penalty spot after 53 minutes after he had been brought down by John Mackie.

The home side pulled a goal back with 15 minutes remaining, as Gary Alexander's downward header from Justin Miller beat goalkeeper Scott Shearer.

Agogo was on target again in the 82nd minute when he latched on to a long ball from James Hunt and ran on to beat his marker before rounding Garner and rolling the ball into an empty net.

Orient scored again in the final minute, through Daryl McMahon who gathered Shearer's punched clearance before drilling a shot into the net through a ruck of players.

Atkins was full of praise for his side afterwards; *'It's the most solid we have looked all season, and we always looked capable of scoring goals.*

'We've won two of our four away games and now have two home games to come, so we have to try and make them count.

'We played well today, and the club goes forward. It's not about individuals, it's about the club.'

Rovers: Shearer, Gibb, Hinton, Anderson, Elliott, Ryan, Disley (Campbell), Hunt, Leary, Walker (Bass), Agogo (Louis).

Substitutes: Carruthers, Forrester

Last Game In Charge

The win at Leyton Orient came after a torrid August in which Rovers lost three of the five games played.

Home draws, against Lincoln City and Oxford United followed, and so Rovers headed off to Chester on September 17th 2005 having not won a home game and languishing in 17th place in the league.

Christian Edwards, who had returned from a loan spell with Swansea, was included on the bench for the game against a side managed by former Rovers defender Keith Curle.

However, Rovers suffered a 4-0 hammering and their performance was greeted with derision by their own fans, two of whom turned their backs on the game in the second half as a protest at what they had seen in the opening period. (pictured)

Rovers held out for 34 minutes and then conceded twice in a minute. Sean Hessey's cross was cleared as far as Ryan Lowe, who fired home from 15 yards, and almost immediately David Artell headed past Scott Shearer from 12 yards.

The home side actually took a three goal lead into the break, as Scott McNiven's cross was headed home by Marcus Richardson in first half stoppage time.

It was a case of damage limitation by Rovers in the second half, but they conceded again with three minutes remaining when Gregg Blundell bundled the ball over the line after Artell's effort had come back into play off the crossbar.

None of the players attended the post-match press conference. Had they done so, they would have heard their manager lay the blame firmly at their door; *'We were beaten up and mugged and conceded three goals in ten minutes, which meant the game was over by half time.*

'We have conceded too many goals since Christmas and yet we still have the same personnel. The three goals we conceded in those ten crazy minutes saw certain players drop their heads because they knew they had made fundamental mistakes.'

Atkins spoke to no one on the team coach, from the time we left the ground to the time we dropped him off in the Midlands and he was relieved of his duties later the following week when a club statement said; *'We served notice to Mr Atkins, on Wednesday, that his contract would not be renewed on expiry of the notice period, and after a training session on Thursday we confirmed that he would not be required to continue his duties, though he remains an employee of the club.'*

Paul Trollope, assisted by John Anderson, was placed in temporary charge for the home game against Darlington on September 24th. It was the start of a new era.

Rovers: Shearer, Hinton, Anderson (Edwards), Elliott, Gibb, Leary (Lescott), Hunt, Campbell (Disley), Carruthers, Walker, Agogo.

Substitutes: Louis, Ryan

The New Management Team

The new, temporary, management team of Paul Trollope and John Anderson faced three games during their first week in charge, beginning with a home match against Darlington on September 24th 2005.

Speaking ahead of the game central defender Craig Hinton, who lived next door to Anderson, said that he might have to start treating his neighbour with a little more respect!

'Maybe I'll have to butter him up with a few extra cups of tea, and I'm not sure if I'll be allowed to travel into training with him any more now he's management!'

Several names were being mentioned as possible replacements for Ian Atkins, among them Keith Curle, Leroy Rosenior, Russell Osman and Exeter's Alex Inglethorpe. However, Rovers' chairman Geoff Dunford said the club would not be rushed into making a decision on a new manager; *'It's early days yet and we will give it a couple of days to see what sort of applications come in, then they will be discussed among the Board of Directors. There is no one lined up, and we won't be discussing what sort of person we are looking for.*

'We have an open mind and we can't rule anything out at this stage. If a manager is at another club and wants to come to Bristol Rovers, then that's not good news for the club involved anyway as it means they have a manager who isn't happy in his employment.'

Trollope and Anderson, who had put his playing career on hold and delayed having an operation to help out, led Rovers to their first home win of the season, as a Richard Walker (pictured) goal gave them all three points in front of a Memorial Stadium crowd of 5,652.

The goal came in first half stoppage time when Aaron Lescott found Junior Agogo and he, in turn, found Walker whose shot was deflected past goalkeeper Sam Russell.

After the game, Trollope wouldn't be drawn into saying he was interested in the manager's job on a full time basis; *'I've not talked about that and I'm not going to do it now.*

'I'm just going to do my job for the next two or three games, with John Anderson alongside me. We have a couple of hard away trips coming up now, but we will have the same preparation and approach and we will see where we are after that.'

Citing man management, or rather a lack of it, during the time Atkins had been in charge, he said; *'The man management of players has probably been the biggest problem at the club and with John, I have someone who knows how they tick. I'm confident that we can get the best out of people.*

'Players have to be treated the right way to play football and that's not something that's happened for the last 18 months.'

Rovers: Shearer, Lescott, Hinton, Elliott, Ryan, Gibb, Leary, Hunt, Carruthers, Agogo, Walker.

Substitutes: Campbell, Anderson, Forrester, Disley, Haldane

First Away Win For 'Trolls'

Three days after their first game under Paul Trollope and John Anderson, Rovers travelled to Gigg Lane, Bury, where they lost 1-0.

Speculation as to who the new manager might be continued, with the local press identifying, rightly or wrongly, Mike Walker, Tommy Taylor, Paul Hart and Ian Holloway among the rumoured 80 applicants for the job.

That didn't bother the temporary management duo, (pictured) though, as they had another long away trip to prepare for, against Carlisle United at Brunton Park, on October 1st 2005.

They returned to Bristol with all three points, thanks to a 3-1 win achieved with the help of two own goals.

And that was after making the worst possible start to the game, as the home side scored their 'consolation goal' after only seven minutes. Craig Hinton slipped when in possession, allowing Alan O'Brien, making his debut after a loan move from Newcastle United, to race clear before beating Scott Shearer with a low shot into the corner of the net.

Still trailing at the break, despite putting in a decent performance, Rovers were back on level terms after 57 minutes. As Junior Agogo and Danny Livesey challenged for the ball in the six yard box, following a punched clearance by goalkeeper Keiren Westwood, the Carlisle defender appeared to touch the ball into his own net.

Eight minutes from time another home defender, Zigor Aranalde attempted to block a shot from Agogo, but the ball deflected off him and flew into the net for another own goal.

Agogo, who had played a part in both of those goals, finally managed to get on the scoresheet himself in the last minute, when he latched on to a through ball from Aaron Lescott and lobbed the ball over Westwood and into the net.

Trollope was delighted with his first win on the road; *'After the first ten minutes I think we were the better side throughout, and I felt we deserved our win.*

'Carlisle put us under pressure right from the kick off by putting the ball in the corner and we worked on ways of getting out of that after our experience at Bury on Tuesday.

'I've got belief in the players and the system we're playing, and I think the players believe in it too.'

He also felt that in strikers Agogo and Richard Walker he had the best strike partnership in the division; *'We weren't set up before to play to Richard's strength, which is to get the ball into his body to enable him to link play. Now we are doing that, and I think he will take off and score a lot of goals.*

'Junior deserves credit because his consistency over the last month has been the best since I joined the club.'

Rovers: Shearer, Lescott, Hinton, Elliott, Carruthers, Gibb, Leary, Hunt, Disley, Walker, Agogo.

Substitutes: Anderson, Forrester, Haldane, Bass, Horsell

Walker At The Double

As we approached the end of October 2005 Paul Trollope and John Anderson remained at the helm as the club sought to bring in a new manager.

October 22nd saw Wrexham visit the Memorial Stadium and, in front of a crowd of 5,730, they were beaten 2-1 thanks to two Richard Walker (pictured) goals.

A fairly even first half ended goalless and then the visitors took the lead after 56 minutes.

Craig Disley conceded a free kick and that was taken by Darren Ferguson, who floated the ball into the box where former Rovers' loan player Danny Williams nodded it on to Dennis Lawrence and he scored from close range.

Despite creating a couple of decent chances, Rovers were unable to get back on level terms and were staring defeat in the face when Richard Walker scored two minutes from time.

Jamie Forrester picked out the striker with a cross from the right and he headed his seventh goal of the season past goalkeeper Michael Ingham.

Incredibly, there was still time for Walker to grab a winner for his side deep into stoppage time. A short corner was played to Stuart Campbell and his cross was met by Walker who again headed home.

Once more Trollope remained tight lipped about whether or not he wanted to be manager on a permanent basis, though he was happy to talk about the dramatic victory that saw his side take all three points; *'It was a triumph for the spirit the lads have shown since I've been in charge.*

'I must admit I was preparing to give a losing address in the dressing room afterwards, but the players stuck at it and produced two good goals.

'I thought Richard Walker was more of a threat than Junior Agogo on the day and that's why I took Junior off near the end. It was a footballing decision and it came off.

'The three substitutes I sent on all affected the game and deserve praise. I think we can start looking upwards towards the play off positions now. It was a very big result for us.'

It was the seventh game that he and John Anderson had been in charge and he made his most unpopular decision to date when he replaced fans favourite Agogo with Lewis Haldane nine minutes from time, when the crowd expected Walker to be substituted.

Jamie Forrester, speaking after the game, said; *'You have to commend Paul for having the guts to make the substitutions he did and the personnel he changed.*

'The crowd weren't too pleased at the time, but look at the outcome. We won the game and Richard Walker scored two fantastic goals. Paul showed bottle making those decisions and he deserves a big pat on the back.'

Rovers: Shearer, Lescott, Hinton, Elliott, Ryan, Gibb (Campbell), Hunt, Disley, Carruthers (Forrester), Agogo (Haldane), Walker.

Substitutes: Anderson, Horsell

Mariners Sunk!

The managerial rumour mill was in overdrive as Rovers prepared for their first round FA Cup tie against Grimsby Town on November 5th 2005.

Although Paul Trollope and John Anderson were still in charge on a temporary basis, they would have read that, in no particular order, Jim Smith, Paul Hart, Frank Burrows, Leroy Rosenior and John Ward were all being put forward as the next incumbent of the Memorial Stadium hot seat.

Two days before the long trip north a new name entered the race for the managerial vacancy for the first time, that of Lennie Lawrence.

It was widely accepted that the Grimsby game would be the last we would see of the caretaker managerial duo of Trollope and Anderson, though many felt that Trollope would be asked to stay on and work alongside a Director of Football.

Whatever lay in store didn't trouble the duo as their side eased past The Mariners, winning 2-1 with both goals being scored by Junior Agogo.

The striker scored the only goal of the first half with 27 minutes on the clock. His first shot, from Richard Walker's cross was blocked by future Rovers goalkeeper Steve Mildenhall, but the ball ran free and Agogo got a final touch to claim his eighth goal of the season.

The home side drew level four minutes into the second half when Gary Jones swept the ball into the net despite Craig Hinton's valiant attempt to stop the ball crossing the line.

The tie was settled five minutes from time. A cross from Chris Carruthers (pictured) was beaten away by Mildenhall, who then blocked a follow up shot from Craig Disley. Once again, though, the loose ball reached Agogo who lashed a shot high into the roof of the net.

It is, perhaps, worth noting that, as well as Mildenhall, there was another future Rovers player in the Grimsby side that day, one JP Kalala.

Speaking after the game, Trollope commented as follows; *'It was fantastic to win.*

'We had a long trip up here and knew it was going to be a very tough game against one of the sides that have been flying in our division.

'We knew when the draw was made that it was going to be a very difficult game, but we came here in a positive frame of mind and got the result I felt we deserved.'

It was, as we shall see, his last post-match press conference as caretaker boss. Two days after the Grimsby match and after Rovers had been handed an away tie at Port Vale in the second round of the FA Cup, he was appointed first team coach on a permanent basis, working alongside a Director of Football.

That man was none other than Lawrence, a former Grimsby manager and a late entrant in the race to become boss.

Rovers: Shearer, Lescott, Hinton, Elliott, Ryan, Gibb (Campbell), Hunt, Disley, Carruthers, Agogo, Walker.

Substitutes: Edwards, Bass, Forrester, Haldane

Lennie And 'Trolls' Take Charge

Monday November 7th 2005 saw Rovers finally end their search for a successor to former manager Ian Atkins.

Lennie Lawrence was named as Director of Football, with former player and caretaker boss Paul Trollope his first team coach and the duo are pictured shortly after being appointed.

The vastly experienced Lawrence had never played league football, but turned out for non league sides Croydon, Carshalton and Sutton United.

His managerial career had taken in Cardiff City, Grimsby Town, Luton Town, Bradford City, Middlesbrough, Charlton Athletic and Plymouth Argyle.

He was adamant that he didn't want to manage again and said that the Director of Football role suited him; 'If someone came in here who was 10 or 15 years younger than me and he really wanted to be a manager and that was obvious, there would be a threat and it wouldn't work.

'But I've been a manager now and I want to see Paul do it and to do what I want to do. I want to run a football club.

'I believe in Directors of Football and I think half the clubs in the Football league need one. Bristol Rovers have been perceptive and honest enough to recognise they probably need one.

'Paul Trollope has the makings of certainly a good coach and possibly a manager as well. I have worked with lots of assistants and young people and I back myself to bring the best out in them.

'Paul has to listen as well, and we have to try and combine my vast experience and knowledge with his youthful enthusiasm.'

To those who knew him, it was obvious that Trollope was destined to be either a manager or a coach. He always credited Jean Tigana, who was his manager when he was at Fulham, as the coach who inspired him and he had kept a record of every training session he had ever seen the Frenchman put on.

His father, John Trollope, was a Swindon Town legend while his own career had seen him start as a youngster at Swindon and then play league football for Torquay United, Derby County, Grimsby Town and Crystal Palace (both on loan), Fulham, Coventry City, Northampton Town and Rovers, while he had also picked up nine full international caps for Wales along the way.

Not surprisingly, his father had been an influence on his career; 'When I got a bit older, he did individual coaching with me and gave me a few ideas. His knowledge of the game and things I picked up from him are helping me now.

'I have also taken things from all the managers I've worked with. When I was a kid at Swindon, I was lucky enough to work with Glenn Hoddle and Ossie Ardiles.

'I've also played under Roy McFarland, Jim Smith, Kevin Keegan, Ray Wilkins and Tigana, so I've been really lucky.

'At Northampton my manager was Colin Calderwood, who was another fantastic boss and someone I'd known since my Swindon days.'

A New Era Begins

While the new management team of Lennie Lawrence and Paul Trollope prepared for the first game following their appointment, news came through of the amount of money Rovers would receive, from Chelsea, for Scott Sinclair.

The promising young footballer had signed for the London club in the summer and a tribunal ruled that the Stamford Bridge outfit should pay £200,000 immediately with clauses included for further payments. For instance, another £50,000 would be paid on his debut for Chelsea's first team, a further £125,000 would become due after 10 first team games, £125,000 after 20 games and the same amount after 30 and 40 games.

In addition, Rovers would receive 15% of any transfer fee received by Chelsea and the club will receive £200,000 if he was ever capped by his country.

A few days later Rochdale visited the Memorial Stadium for the first game of a new era for Rovers and, as so often happens when an occasion is built up, it all went wrong. A crowd of 6,042 turned up hoping for a Rovers win but saw the visitors claim all three points with a 2-1 win that left their side in 18th place in the league table.

The Rochdale lineup makes interesting reading as a certain Rickie Lambert, later a player of this parish and later of Southampton and England fame, could only make the bench, along with former Rovers striker Paul Tait.

Grant Holt was their main striker that afternoon and he opened the scoring after 12 minutes when he beat Scott Shearer from the penalty spot after Robbie Ryan was adjudged to have fouled Lee Cartwright.

Rovers were back on level terms by half time, though, as Junior Agogo collected Richard Walker's knockdown and beat goalkeeper Matthew Gilks from 15 yards.

The winning goal came on 64 minutes when the unmarked Blair Sturrock collected a cross from Cartwright and scored from close range.

Michael Leary is pictured sandwiched between two Rochdale defenders.

If anyone thought they might hear from the newly appointed Director of Football afterwards, they were disappointed as Trollope came to face the press, and that's the way it remained during the time the two of them were in charge.

The first team coach said; *'I've been told I will have final say in team selection and tactics, which is great as far as I'm concerned.*

'Lennie has had a big input before the game, at half time and in the dressing room afterwards. I'm glad to say our views on the game are very similar, as are our opinions on how football should be played.'

As for the game, he had this to say; *'I thought the lads deserved a point, but there were no complaints about the penalty. However, I felt we dropped a bit deep in midfield at times, which is something we will be working on.'*

Rovers: Shearer, Lescott, Hinton, Elliott, Ryan, Campbell, Leary, Disley, Carruthers (Forrester), Walker (Haldane), Agogo.

Substitutes: Horsell, Edwards, Bass

Bees Beaten

A first win under Lennie Lawrence and Paul Trollope was achieved on November 26th 2005, just a week after the side had suffered a mauling at the hands of Northampton Town, going down 4-0 at Sixfields.

The visitors to the Memorial Stadium that afternoon were Barnet, the team we had drawn against on the opening day of the season.

Just over 5,000 fans were there to see Richard Walker score two first half goals, though Rovers weren't able to add to their tally after the break.

The striker scored his first after only four minutes when James Hunt's pass split the Barnet defence allowing him to pick his spot and drive the ball past Ross Flitney from 15 yards.

The second arrived on the 20 minute mark, but this time Stuart Campbell was the supplier, picking out Walker with a pinpoint pass. The striker made the most of the opportunity and fired his second goal of the afternoon past Flitney.

With former Rovers striker Giuliano Grazioli leading their attack, the visitors began to dominate possession and it came as little surprise when they managed to pull a goal back after 67 minutes.

A corner taken by a player whose Rovers career had lasted barely a minute (in the final game of the previous season), Louie Soares, sent a corner into the area where Ben Strevens was first to react and he headed past Scott Shearer.

On the bench that afternoon was central defender Christian Edwards, who had thought his Rovers career was over after being transfer listed by former manager Ian Atkins and sidelined by illness and injury for three months. *'I'm feeling really sharp in training and I think the rest has done me good, though it's been a really frustrating time for me because I'm not a good watcher.*

'I'm fresher and fitter than I've been in ages and I can't wait for the opportunity to get back in the side.'

Extensive hospital tests, undertaken after he began suffering blackouts, had revealed nothing untoward; *'It was a worrying time for me, and I wasn't sure what the future would hold. Fortunately, the tests proved there was nothing seriously wrong and that came as a huge relief.*

'I want to get back in the side and repay Paul Trollope for the faith he's shown in me.'

As for the Barnet game, another central defender, Craig Hinton (pictured), had this to say; *'We felt a bit of pressure going into the game, probably because of where we were in the table.*

'Beating them has lifted a weight from our shoulders and we'll go to Port Vale (in the FA Cup) *without any pressure on us.*

'It's important we build on the win and put a run of results together. We need to push on from where we are and, if we can get back to back wins, it could kickstart our season.'

Rovers: Shearer, Carruthers, Elliott, Hinton, Lescott, Campbell, Hunt, Disley (Leary), Gibb, Walker (Haldane), Agogo.

Substitutes: Edwards, Forrester, Horsell

Walker On The Spot

Rovers travelled to Edgeley Park, to take on Stockport County, on 6th December 2005 looking to record back to back wins in the league for the first time in 15 months.

Barnet had been beaten two weeks earlier and that was followed by a 1-1 draw against Port Vale in the second round of the FA Cup at Vale Park.

Rovers travelled to the north west with two former Stockport players in their squad, namely Ali Gibb and Aaron Lescott (pictured)

Gibb, in particular, was looking forward to facing his former club, saying; *'I had four years with the club and really enjoyed it, although it's a totally different club now to when I was there.*

'I still know a few people there but now I just want to go back and do well with Bristol Rovers. I wasn't that surprised at what has happened to them because I think people could see what was coming when money was taken out of the club.

'For various reasons, football stopped being a priority there with a takeover in the background and, although what's happened to them isn't surprising, it's still very sad.'

In a scrappy game, Rovers managed to take all three points, courtesy of Richard Walker's first half penalty, and inflict a first home defeat of the season on County.

Stockport's Jermaine Easter, a future Rovers player, had the ball in the net after only five minutes, but his effort was ruled out by an offside decision.

It then needed a superb save by goalkeeper Scott Shearer, from Matthew Hamshaw, to keep Rovers on level terms and it took them almost 20 minutes before they managed a goal attempt of their own, but Craig Disley's header drifted harmlessly wide of the upright.

They scored what proved to be the winning goal with 35 minutes on the clock when Gibb's cross from the right was adjudged to have been handled by defender Danny Boshell, though many thought it had hit him in the face.

There was no changing referee Graham Salisbury's mind, though, and Walker sent goalkeeper James Spencer the wrong way from the penalty spot.

Chances were at a premium for both sides in the second half. Easter twice went close to equalising for Stockport, hitting the side netting with one effort before squandering a gilt edged opportunity when he headed wide shortly afterwards.

Junior Agogo saw a shot saved by Spencer with his legs and Shearer again came to Rovers rescue a minute from time when he saved from Michael Malcolm.

After the game Walker revealed that he had a £100 bet with Agogo as to who would finish the season as top scorer and that the two would alternate on penalties; *"I'm one ahead of him now, and if he wants to raise the stakes it's up to him. I know I'm going to win, anyway, so there's no rush!"*

Rovers: Shearer, Lescott, Hinton, Elliott, Carruthers, Gibb, Hunt, Disley, Campbell, Walker, Agogo.

Substitutes: Edwards, Forrester, Leary, Williams, Book.

Hart On Losing Side At The Mem

Boxing Day 2005 saw Shrewsbury Town visit the Memorial Stadium, where a crowd of 7,551 saw them beaten 2-1 by Rovers.

In goal for the Shrews was the future England and Manchester City goalkeeper Joe Hart (pictured facing up to Junior Agogo), who was beaten by Craig Disley and Agogo as Rovers moved into tenth place in the league standings.

A one minute's silence was observed prior to kick off in memory of former kitman Ray Kendall, who had passed away on Christmas Eve and that was followed by a very loud rendition of the club's theme song, 'Goodnight Irene'.

Among the tributes paid to Ray was this one from Chairman Geoff Dunford; *'Ray was Mr Bristol Rovers. He was a real gentleman and worked for the club for more than 50 years. He was a real character and had stories to tell from his many years here that always kept us amused. He dedicated his life to the football club, and it was as though he was married to it. We are all going to miss him greatly. A little part of Bristol Rovers has gone today and will never be replaced.'*

Kendall would, no doubt, have been delighted that his beloved Rovers picked up three points that afternoon, though it has to be said they struggled to achieve victory even though they took a two goal lead into the half time interval.

Disley opened the scoring after 35 minutes. When a back heeled attempt from Junior Agogo was blocked on the line, the ball rebounded to the midfielder who nodded it into the net from a yard out.

Rovers were awarded a penalty in first half stoppage time after Steve Elliott, up for a corner, was held back by defender Richard Hope. The resulting spot kick saw Junior Agogo send Hart the wrong way to give his side a comfortable half time lead.

However, the visitors pulled a goal back four minutes into the second half when Duane Darby met a cross from Kelvin Langmead and beat Scott Shearer with a shot high into the net from six yards.

Hart, then a teenager, distinguished himself with a save, at the second attempt, from Agogo and Rovers survived a few anxious moments before the 90 minutes were up and again in the four minutes of added time.

Their reward for victory was an iced bath and Paul Trollope explained the reasoning behind a not entirely welcome move; *'The players went into the iced bath for one minute then had a warm shower before spending another two minutes in the iced bath. It's a recovery technique used quite a lot by rugby players and, apparently, it can aid recovery time by 25%. I've told the players that it's not a punishment for anything and that it will help our preparations for the hectic holiday period.'*

Rovers: Shearer, Lescott, Hinton, Elliott, Carruthers, Gibb, Hunt, Disley, Campbell, Walker, Agogo (Forrester).

Substitutes: Edwards, Williams, Haldane, Book.

Happy New Year

Although they ended 2005 with a 2-1 home defeat at the hands of Wycombe Wanderers on New Year's Eve, Rovers kicked of 2006 in style by registering a 3-2 win against Rushden & Diamonds on January 2nd.

They went into the game without Ryan Williams, whose contract had expired at the end of December and who had rejected the offer of a new six month contract in favour of joining Aldershot. With the benefit of hindsight, it wasn't his best ever career move!

Paul Trollope said of the diminutive midfielder's departure; *'We are going to miss him in the squad because he gave us something a bit different. We felt a six month deal gave him a chance to stay at the football club but, unfortunately, we weren't in a position to offer him anything longer. It's very disappointing.'*

The game at Nene Park provided great entertainment, with the crowd of 2,720 witnessing five goals and two red, and five yellow cards.

Both sides were reduced to ten men, with the game still goalless, on 37 minutes following James Hunt's late challenge on Alun Armstrong who reacted by getting to his feet and pushing the Rovers skipper in the back. Referee Tony Bates was quick to send both players off.

Three minutes later Rovers were ahead when Stuart Campbell hit a 25 yard free kick into the area that was missed by everyone. The ball ended up in the far corner of the net for his first ever Rovers' goal. He didn't score many, so this was a real collector's item!

The home side levelled just a minute later as Drewe Broughton nodded the ball past Scott Shearer, playing against his former club, from an Andy Burgess cross.

Three minutes into the second half Steve Elliott restored Rovers lead when he fired home from ten yards after goalkeeper Jamie Young spilt a shot from Campbell.

There were six minutes remaining when Broughton levelled the score with his second goal of the afternoon. The big striker received the ball with his back to goal and was allowed time and space to turn before hitting a low shot into the corner of the net.

Deep into stoppage time, and just when it seemed that Rovers would have to settle for a point, Jamie Forrester, pictured being congratulated by Steve Elliott and Craig Disley, met Richard Walker's cross and headed past Young from six yards to earn Rovers their seventh point from their four holiday fixtures.

The win moved Rovers up to eighth place and Elliott said this of his second goal of the season; *'To be honest, I didn't think I'd ever score a goal with my right foot, but I just hit it and it went in the corner. I've set myself a target of five goals for the season and it was good to get another one under my belt.'*

Rovers: Shearer, Lescott, Hinton, Elliott, Carruthers, Forrester, Hunt, Disley, Campbell, Walker, Haldane (Gibb).

Substitutes: Edwards, Anderson, Lines, Book

Another Late Victory

There were 12 days between the 3-2 win against Rushden & Diamonds and the next league fixture, against Cheltenham Town at Whaddon Road.

In that time Rovers had signed Millwall midfielder Sammy Igoe on a month's loan, shortly after handing defender Jon Bass a contract until the end of the season.

I have good reason to remember this particular game at Cheltenham, because it was the first of three games in which I acted as kitman while Roger Harding was in France looking after his wife, Pat, who had been taken ill whilst on a short break.

Rovers recorded another 3-2 win, with yet another late, late, goal but unfortunately I didn't see our first of the afternoon.

Defender Craig Hinton caught an elbow in the eye in the first minute of the game and needed to come off. It was an injury that required a hospital visit, so I was detailed to sit in the dressing room with him while we waited for an ambulance.

It's quite eerie sitting in a changing room listening to the crowd and wondering what an earth is going on, but there was no mistaking the fact that Rovers had taken the lead after 18 minutes when Jamie Forrester's free kick beat former Rovers' goalkeeper Shane Higgs.

The noise was deafening inside the broom cupboard that, at that time, doubled as the away changing room at Whaddon Road and even Hinton, although semi conscious, celebrated after a fashion!

Once he had left for the hospital. I returned to the bench and saw Steven Gillespie, later a Rovers player, of course, level the scores on 69 minutes.

With three minutes remaining Kayode Odejayi headed the home side in front and all, apart from the 1,675 Rovers fans in the crowd of 6,005 thought that was it. They reckoned without Craig Disley and John Anderson, though.

Disley headed in from Junior Agogo's cross straight after Cheltenham's second goal and then, deep into stoppage time, Anderson glanced the ball beyond Higgs from Stuart Campbell's ball into the box.

Cue pandemonium and elation, and that was only on the bench!

The photo shows Anderson (number 14) being congratulated by his delighted team mates!

Disley, whose equaliser was his fourth of the season, said; *'I thought the game had gone when they went 2-1 up so late on, but I managed to pop up with a goal from our next attack and we got that belief back again.*

'It was a fantastic finish to the game for us to get the winner and you only had to look at the reaction of the players and the fans to see what it meant to people.'

Rovers: Shearer, Lescott, Edwards, Hinton (Anderson), Carruthers, Campbell, Disley, Gibb (Igoe), Walker, Haldane (Agogo), Forrester.

Substitutes: Mullings, Book

Costly Penalty Miss

Rovers were in tenth place going into their home game against Leyton Orient on January 31st 2006, a position they stayed in following an entertaining 3-3 draw.

They gained their point the hard way, having to fight back from behind on two occasions.

There was a Memorial Stadium crowd of only 5,966 to see the 90th league meeting between the clubs, but they were treated to a thrilling evening's entertainment. Junior Agogo set the ball rolling with a goal after 14 minutes when he latched on to Sammy Igoe's superb through ball and although his first shot was parried by goalkeeper Glyn Garner, the striker drilled the loose ball into the net from ten yards.

It was no more than Rovers deserved as they completely dominated first half proceedings. In fact, they should have been two goals to the good at the break but Agogo's stoppage time penalty, awarded after Stuart Campbell was fouled by Justin Miller, was saved by Garner.

Jabo Ibehre, on as a second half substitute, scored an equaliser for the O's two minutes after the restart when he lashed the ball high into the roof of the net from close range following Daryl McMahon's free kick.

Nine minutes later the same player gave his side the lead when he beat Steve Elliott to a long clearance and lobbed the ball over the advancing Scott Shearer.

The visitors held the lead for just two minutes and conceded an equaliser when Richard Walker and Garner attempted to reach a free kick played into the box. However, both missed it and it fell to Craig Disley, who headed home from close range.

Orient were back in front after another three minutes when Michael Simpson glanced a header past Shearer from Shane Tudor's cross.

The scoring was completed on 71 minutes when Rovers were awarded their second penalty of the evening after Christian Edwards was fouled in the area. Walker (pictured) assumed responsibility for this spot kick and blasted the ball high into the roof of the net as Garner dived to his right.

The 3-3 scoreline meant that 20 goals had been scored, and ten points gained, in the club's five January fixtures.

After the match, Paul Trollope revealed he wasn't a fan of Agogo and Walker alternating with any penalties that might be awarded in future games; *'Having one regular penalty taker is something both Lennie Lawrence and myself would like to see and it's something we can hopefully address this week.'*

In fact, the matter was resolved almost immediately, as Walker was quick to point out; *'Penalties are down to me now. Junior and I had been taking them in turn, but we had agreed beforehand that if anyone missed the other would carry on with the job. That's what we decided and that's what we are sticking to, so now it's down to me until I miss one.'*

Rovers: Shearer, Lescott (Anderson), Edwards, Elliott, Carruthers, Igoe, Hunt, Disley, Campbell, Agogo, Walker.

Substitutes: Lines, Haldane, Mullings, Book

A Posh Win

A 5-0 home win for the reserves, against Swindon Town, preceded a trip to London Road, Peterborough for a League Two clash on February 25th 2006.

On target for the second string were Lewis Haldane, Sammy Igoe, Chris Lines, Matt Groves and Swindon's Steve Jenkins, who put through his own net.

Aaron Lescott, Craig Hinton, John Anderson and Robbie Ryan were all included in the reserves for the match, and of that quartet only Hinton made the starting lineup against Peterborough.

Haldane (pictured) was also recalled to the first team, but Igoe missed out after sustaining an injury in the reserve team clash against his former club.

It was the third meeting of the sides that season, with Peterborough having triumphed in the league fixture at the Memorial Stadium and in the LDV Vans Trophy tie played at London Road in October 2005.

Rovers though, came out on top on this occasion thanks to the quite formidable strike partnership of Junior Agogo and Richard Walker.

Agogo scored the opener on 36 minutes when he picked up on a long ball played out from the back by James Hunt. He shrugged off a challenge from former Rovers loanee Chris Plummer and fired a shot past goalkeeper Lee Harrison, who managed to get a hand to the ball but couldn't prevent it going into the net.

Walker doubled the lead ten minutes into the second half when he headed past Harrison following Stuart Campbell's free kick.

A minute later Rovers were reduced to ten men when Agogo was red carded for, apparently, kicking out at defender Phil Bolland.

The home side, though, failed to make their numerical superiority count and it wasn't until the last minute of the game that they scored what was to be a mere consolation.

The scorer, Dean Holden, managed to beat Scott Shearer from close range, but it wasn't enough to prevent his side's first home defeat since the previous September.

First Team Coach Paul Trollope felt the winning margin could have been greater; *'We could possibly have won more comfortably than we did, and it was disappointing to concede right at the end because it took the gloss off a magnificent team performance.*

'But to be fair to Peterborough they kept going and nicked a goal to make things tense for a minute or so.'

Of the sending off, Trollope said; *'It was a strange incident, and we didn't think too much happened. We'll need to look at it again, but their defender and goalkeeper said that Junior didn't do anything, which is a positive for us.*

'The referee said that Junior had kicked out at Bolland after he had been pushed in the back.'

Rovers: Shearer, Bass, Hinton, Elliott, Carruthers, Haldane, Hunt, Disley, Campbell, Walker, Agogo.

Substitutes: Edwards, Forrester, Lescott, Mullings, Book

Stags Sent Packing

March 2006 began with Rovers sitting just four points and two places outside the play off positions, but the game scheduled to be played against Oxford United on March 4th was called off because of the frozen state of the Kassam Stadium pitch.

The postponement seemed to affect Paul Trollope's side as they then lost three consecutive league games, against Notts County at the Memorial Stadium, the rearranged game at Oxford, and at Shrewsbury Town.

The home defeat at the hands of Notts County, incidentally, saw goalkeeper Steve Book play his one and only league game for Rovers when he replaced the injured Scott Shearer just half an hour before kick off after the former Coventry and Rushden & Diamonds shot stopper suffered from back spasms.

The final game of the month saw Mansfield Town visit the Memorial Stadium, where Paul Trollope's side had won only six out of 18 games all season.

Striker Jamie Forrester had gone out on loan, to Lincoln City, in the week leading up to the game but he didn't seem to be missed as goals from Sammy Igoe, his first for the club, and Richard Walker (pictured) sealed a comfortable victory.

Igoe's goal came after 14 minutes when Lewis Haldane's cross from the right was only half cleared and when the ball reached Igoe he drilled it past goalkeeper Kevin Pressman from twenty yards.

Three minutes later Walker doubled the advantage after he ran on to Igoe's through ball and rounded Pressman before hitting the back of the net with an angled drive.

There were no further goals for the home crowd of 5,253 to cheer as both sides found difficulty coping with a pitch that resembled a ploughed field in some areas after heavy rain fell during the match.

Victory left Rovers three points outside the top seven and renewed hopes of a play off place come the end of the season, and Trollope said; *'We know that with three points in it and things so tight, it can all change over the space of one Saturday.'*

Of the win against Mansfield, he added; *'We came out of the traps probably better than we have all season. We've come at teams strongly in matches if we've gone a goal down, and this time I asked the players to start like that and we created a good tempo.*

'There was pressure on because we didn't want to lose another one. We knew our home form in recent weeks hadn't been great but what pleased me was that there wasn't an uncomfortable 20 minutes or anxious end to the game, and we looked quite comfortable.'

Trollope praised the work of his strikers, Walker and Junior Agogo; *'They were the catalyst right from the start. They are our talismen and set the tone for us if they are working hard.'*

Rovers: Shearer, Lescott, Hinton, Elliott, Carruthers, Haldane, Hunt, Disley, Igoe, Walker, Agogo (Gibb).

Substitutes: Edwards, Lines, Bass, Horsell

Winners at Wycombe

Play off aspirations rose once again after a 3-1 win against Wycombe Wanderers at the then named Causeway Stadium on April 1st 2006.

Victory saw Rovers occupying ninth place, but level on points with the two teams immediately above them, Lincoln City and Peterborough United.

There was one player looking forward to the game against Wycombe more than most.

Defender Chris Carruthers (pictured), a former England Youth international, had agreed a deal with the Chairboys only to have a last minute change of heart after receiving a call from Rovers. He had spent two months on loan with Rovers before agreeing to join Wycombe and then decided to move to the Memorial Stadium rather than the Causeway Stadium; 'I actually signed for Wycombe at the end of last season because I was told that Rovers couldn't offer me anything. But then I got a call from Rovers saying that there was an offer on the table after all, so I changed my mind and came here. I changed my mind because I knew the manager and the players at Rovers and I knew there was a good team here with a chance of pushing on, so I have no regrets.'

The win against Wycombe was, not surprisingly, achieved with goals from Junior Agogo and Richard Walker.

Agogo gave his side the lead just after the half hour mark, beating goalkeeper Frank Talia from 12 yards after defender Mike Williamson hesitated when trying to deal with Sammy Igoe's cross.

Eight minutes into the second half Walker scored Rovers' second goal from the penalty spot after Craig Disley had been brought down by Williamson. He drove his spot kick straight down the middle, giving Talia no chance of saving.

Agogo made the game safe for Paul Trollope's side on 74 minutes. When he was played in by Igoe, he outpaced everyone before taking the ball round Talia and rolling it into an empty net.

Wycombe, who included future Rovers defender Danny Senda in their lineup, did manage a consolation goal through Jermaine Easter, another future Rovers player, nine minutes from time when he slipped the ball past Scott Shearer following Tommy Mooney's cross.

Trollope was delighted with the victory but played down talk of achieving a play off spot; 'That performance was on a par with our away wins at Grimsby and Peterborough.

'There were a lot of good individual performances, but collectively I thought it was a very good team performance. Junior deserved his goals and I think you always get what you deserve in football. He has worked hard in training all week and was rewarded with those goals. As for the play offs, it's tight and while we have shown before that we are capable of winning three games on the spin, we are also capable of losing three.'

Rovers: Shearer, Lescott, Hinton, Elliott, Carruthers (Edwards), Haldane (Gibb), Hunt, Igoe (Campbell), Disley, Walker, Agogo.

Substitutes: Lines, Horsell

Boston Beaten

Defeat at Wrexham on Easter Monday 2006 all but ended any hopes of Rovers reaching a play off place come the end of the season.

Paul Trollope admitted as much as his side prepared for their penultimate home game of the season against Boston United. With only three games left to play, his side were four points adrift of the top seven; *'We are going flat out for three wins and although our results over the Easter weekend were disappointing (they had also drawn 1-1 against Carlisle United at the Memorial Stadium) we were pleased with much of what we saw.*

'If we can win three on the spin, as we have in the past, then you never know, but we do almost need a miracle to achieve a play off spot.'

Supporters appeared to have given up on miracles, though, as the lowest home crowd of the season, 4,836, turned out to see Rovers achieve a 3-1 win against Boston.

They were ahead on 26 minutes after Richard Walker found Junior Agogo in space out on the right and his cross into the box was met by Craig Disley (pictured) who fired in from five yards.

The visitors levelled on the hour mark when Jamie Clarke nodded on a cross from Chris Holland and Julian Joachim headed in from close range.

Two goals in the space of five minutes then saw Rovers clinch a vital three points. Walker grabbed his side's second of the afternoon, beating on loan goalkeeper Conrad Logan, a future Rovers loanee, from the penalty spot after Lewis Haldane was fouled by Austin McCann.

That was after 72 minutes and Junior Agogo wrapped things up on 77 minutes when he was played in by Disley and hit a terrific shot over Logan to score what was the best goal of the game by far.

Disley's goal was his eighth of the campaign, Walker moved on to 21 and Agogo to 18 and victory left Rovers just two points off a top seven spot with only games against Rochdale (away) and Macclesfield (home) to follow.

Trollope was happy that his side was still in contention; *'All our focus now is on preparations for Rochdale, so the players know what is required.*

'We have to concentrate on our performance in the next game and not what's going on around us.

'Prior to this game we'd had two decent performances with little return, and we said we would take an ugly win. I wouldn't say this was ugly, but we have played better and lost. We had a bit of luck along the way but, in the end, I thought we deserved the win.

'We came in at half time and knew we could improve, which we did, though a poor bit of defending cost us a goal.'

Rovers: Shearer, Lescott, Hinton, Elliott, Carruthers, Hunt, Campbell, Disley, Agogo, Walker, Haldane.

Substitutes: Edwards, Gibb, Lines, Mullings, Horsell

Last Day Defeat

Any lingering hopes Rovers had of reaching the end of season play offs were extinguished by a 2-0 defeat at Spotland, home of Rochdale, on April 29th 2006.

Goals from Rickie Lambert, soon to be a Rovers player, of course, and the late Ernie Cooksey, who was to succumb to cancer in July 2008 at the age of 28 gave the home side victory.

One week later Rovers played their final league game of the season, against Macclesfield Town at the Memorial Stadium. The fixture came after a week that had seen Steve McClaren, assistant manager at Derby County when Paul Trollope was a player there, appointed to the post of England manager.

Rovers went into the Macclesfield game on 60 points, the same total they had finished on in the previous season. A win or a draw would see them finish with their highest total since 2001/02.

Chris Lines made his first start for the club but ended up on the losing side as the visitors left Bristol with all three points following a 3-2 win.

David Morley's close range header, from Kevin McIntyre's corner gave the Silkmen a seventh minute lead, but Lewis Haldane volleyed past goalkeeper Alan Fettis five minutes later to equalise for Rovers.

Marcus Richardson scored a second for Macclesfield, on 28 minutes, after a hesitant Rovers defence failed to deal with Paul Harsley's cross and they held that lead going into the half time interval.

Haldane (pictured) scored his, and Rovers', second goal of the game after 56 minutes when he beat Fettis following a cross from Chris Carruthers.

Two minutes from time, though, Richardson scored again for Macclesfield when he beat Scott Shearer with a close range header.

After the game Trollope admitted that there had been some harsh words in the dressing room at half time; *'In many ways it was a performance that summed up our season as, once again, we started slowly and gave ourselves an uphill battle.*

'I thought we were pretty poor in the first half but, to be fair, the lads responded to what was said during the half time interval.

'We improved for large spells of the second half, but our defensive frailty cost us another game. We are simply not good enough defensively, either individually or as a team. The winning goal showed that.'

At the Supporters Club Awards evening 24 hours later, Walker collected the Player of the Year Award, with Haldane collecting the Young Player of the Year Award.

Already, though, there was speculation about who might be joining the club for the following season, and who could be on their way out of the Memorial Stadium.

Bristol City goalkeeper Steve Phillips was rumoured to be a transfer target, as was Bath City winger Andy Sandell. However, it was thought that several players, including John Anderson and Christian Edwards, had kicked their last ball for the club.

Rovers: Shearer, Lescott, Edwards, Elliott, Carruthers, Disley, Lines (Campbell), Hunt, Haldane, Walker, Agogo.

Substitutes: Gibb, Bass, Mullings, Horsell

PHOTO INDEX –
Listed by Player/Manager/Director

Player	Page Number
Agogo, Junior	41, 45, 56, 58, 62, 72, 74, 79, 92
Anderson, John	53, 85, 94
Astafjevs, Vitalijs	30, 34
Atkins, Ian	57
Barrett, Adam	28, 38, 49, 55
Bater, Phil	18, 51
Beswetherick, Jon	78
Boxall, Danny	42
Broadhurst, Kevan	52, 57
Bubb, Alvin	1
Burns, Steve	52
Cameron, Martin	2
Campbell, Stuart	64, 93
Carlisle, Wayne	30, 44
Carruthers, Chris	87, 94, 98
Cash, Brian	69
Craig, Ron	9
Di Piedi, Michelle	35
Disley, Craig	67, 72, 73, 81, 82, 93, 94, 99
Dunford, Geoff	7, 9, 34
Edwards, Christian	41, 42, 59, 66, 94
Elliott, Steve	80, 93
Ellington, Nathan	6, 8, 10, 13, 14
Foran, Mark	11
Forrester, Jamie	61, 93
Francis, Gerry	1, 7
Gall, Kevin	3
Gibb, Ali	54, 91
Gilroy, David	31, 42
Graydon, Ray	20, 40
Grazioli, Giuliano	21, 23, 25
Greaves, Danny	42
Haldane, Lewis	46, 49, 93, 96, 100
Henriksen, Bo	53
Hinton	90
Hobbs, Shane	42
Hodges, Lee	43

101

Howie, Scott	5
Hunt, James	65, 71, 99
Igoe, Sammy	94
Jeannin, Alex	77
Kite, Phil	18
Lawrence, Lennie	88
Leary, Michael	89
Lee, David	27
Lescott, Aaron	75, 91, 94
Lopez, Rick	19
Louis, Jefferson	79
Matthews, Lee	50
Miller, Kevin	41
Ommel	11, 12
Osman, Russell	52, 57
Parker, Sonny	42
Plummer, Chris	28
Pritchard, David	18
Quinn, Rob	26, 33, 44
Rammell, Andy	36, 37, 39
Tony Ricketts	51
Ross, Neil	4
Ryan, Robbie	80
Sanchez-Lopez, Carlos	19
Savage, Dave	41, 42, 47, 64
Shearer, Scott	93, 94
Sinclair, Scott	68
Still, John	20
Stokes, Vernon	7
Street, Kevin	32, 42
Tait, Paul	22, 24, 25, 29
Thomas, Jamie	17
Thompson, Garry	9, 15
Thorpe, Lee	55, 60, 70
Trollope, Paul	85, 88
Toner, Ciaran	16
Walker, Richard	75, 76, 81, 84, 86, 95, 97
Ward, Elliott	69
Weare, Ross	1
Williams, Danny	53
Williams, Ryan	48, 77, 80, 81
Wilson, Che	11
Wilson, Kevin	15